GOD'S WOUNDS

THE REMARKABLE TRUTH OF THOSE WHO BORE THE SIGNS OF CHRIST'S PASSION

JOHN CLARK

Published by Catholic Answers, Inc.
2020 Gillespie Way
El Cajon, California 92020
1-888-291-8000 orders
619-387-0042 fax
catholic.com

Printed in the United States of America

Cover design by Shane Riter
Interior design by Shawna Kunz | Lime Design | shawna@limedesign.co

978-1-68357-384-5
978-1-68357-385-2 Kindle
978-1-68357-386-9 ePub

DEDICATION

This book is dedicated to my dad, Bruce Thomas Clark.

My father was raised as a Protestant, but quickly fell in love with a young Irish Catholic girl named Mary Katherine, so he began investigating the Catholic faith.

At first, my dad failed to see why the Catholic faith should be considered the One, True Faith. So he asked a priest why the Catholic faith was superior to Protestantism.

The priest asked my dad, "Some Catholics have received the stigmata. Which of the Protestants had the stigmata?"

My dad replied, "What? What's the stigmata?"

The priest explained the stigmata to my dad, pointing to a living stigmatist, Padre Pio.

That was a major turning point in my dad's conversion. After investigating the mystery of the stigmata, my father was convinced that the Catholic faith was the One, True Faith.

I wish I had written this book when my dad was still on earth; surely, he would have loved it. But in heaven, he no longer needs this book for evidence, for he can walk among the sainted stigmatists as friends for eternity.

We know that the apostle Thomas doubted, until he put his hand into the side of Christ. Bruce Thomas no longer has any doubt.

For now, he can put his own hand in the side of Christ and feel the very heartbeat of God.

CONTENTS

PREFACE

This book began almost by accident.

Several years ago, as a regular contributor for Fr. Robert Spitzer's *Magis Center*, I wrote a series of articles explaining C.S. Lewis's fascinating Christological argument often referred to as the "trilemma." In his book *Mere Christianity*, C.S. Lewis explains that some people believe that Jesus was a good man with important teachings, but clearly not God. Lewis, however, argues that the *good man* argument is untenable:

> I am trying here to prevent anyone saying the really foolish thing that people often say about him: "I'm ready to accept Jesus as a great moral teacher, but I don't accept his claim to be God." That is the one thing we must not say. A man who was merely a man and said the sort of things Jesus said would not be a great moral teacher. He would either be a lunatic—on a level with the man who says he is a poached egg—or else he would be the Devil of Hell. You must make your choice. Either this man was, and is, the Son of God: or else a madman or something worse. You can shut him up for a fool, you can spit at him and kill him as a demon; or you can fall at his feet and call him Lord and God. But let us not come with any patronizing nonsense about his being a great human teacher. He has not left that open to us. He did not intend to.[1]

Simply put, in claiming to be God—which Jesus most certainly did—there are three essential possibilities. Either

Jesus was a liar, a lunatic, or Lord. It's terribly logical: no truthful and sane person could claim to be God, and still be a good man—unless, of course, that person *is* God.

Lewis's trilemma is a fascinating argument because it is airtight—liar, lunatic, or Lord—there is no fourth possibility. The trilemma is well known within Catholic apologetics circles, but I didn't feel it was appreciated quite enough. Because beyond the subject matter, what is also profound about Lewis's trilemma is the methodology itself. That is, a trilemma methodology can be logically applied to some other areas of the Catholic faith—and one of those areas is the stigmata. The subject of the stigmata has confounded medical experts, scientists, and skeptics for many centuries. Fr. John Hardon defines *stigmata* as a "phenomenon in which a person bears all or some of the wounds of Christ in his or her own body, i.e., on the feet, hands, side, and brow. The wounds appear spontaneously, from no external source, and periodically there is a flow of fresh blood."[2] Believers and skeptics alike should be able to agree that this is a momentous claim—that the wounds of Jesus suddenly appeared on his or her own body. To determine the veracity of such a claim, we can apply Lewis's trilemma. Even before we investigate any facts, we can conclude that a person who bears such wounds is either a 1) liar, 2) lunatic, or 3) *stigmatist*—that is, one who miraculously bears the wounds of the Savior.

Which is it? For surely, it is one of those three.

After I finished these articles for the *Magis Center* about Lewis's trilemma, I began to assemble research for the stigmata. I originally intended to write three articles in the series about the stigmata, but the more research I did, the more I realized that three articles were not enough. I contacted my editor and told her that it might be more like four or five, but I soon realized that this was not enough either.

By the time I reached eight articles, I realized that I had a book on my hands.

> I had intended to focus primarily on the trilemma methodology itself, but something happened along the way: I began to fall in love with these stigmatists. The more hundreds of hours I spent reading their biographies—St. Lutgarde, St. Catherine of Siena, St. Teresa of Ávila, St. Rita, St. Faustina—the deeper affection I felt for them. True to the reality of the communion of saints, we developed a friendship. For there is no doubt in my heart that these stigmatists prayed for me as I wrote. My good friend Patrick O'Hearn wrote a beautiful and touching book called *Parents of the Saints* a few years ago. In that book, Patrick writes, "I felt more and more saints whisper to me in prayer, 'Tell my parents' story. The world needs to know about our unsung heroes, who laid the foundation for our spiritual lives.'"[3] As I researched and wrote about the stigmatists, I continually sensed a similar message: tell our stories.

Something else happened: I saw the crucifix in a new way. I would not say that I saw the crucifix *differently*, but I began to see it *more completely*. I hope and pray that the reader will have a similar experience. The Sorrowful Mysteries came alive for me during this book. As you will see, those mysteries are a chief focus of this book.

My great hope for this book is that it edifies the faith of the faithful, counsels the doubtful, and speaks to those who do not yet know Christ. There is no greater image of Christ's love for us than the crucifix, for it was on that cross that Christ laid down his life for his friends, and for those he willed to befriend.

In the second half of this book, I do return to my original mission to lay out the apologetics of the trilemma, as it applies to the stigmatists. Before we begin this inquiry into the stigmata and those who claim to bear the stigmata, let us manage expectations and state some ground rules for apologetics. When Catholic apologists discuss the subject of miracles (or from the perspective of a skeptic, those things *purported* to be miracles) such as the eucharistic miracle at Lanciano, the Shroud of Turin, the incorruptibility of St. Bernadette—the audience often demands proof. In fact, the audience often demands the sort of proof that eliminates any possibility to the contrary. Otherwise, it is deemed that the apologist has failed to make his case.

But is that a fair demand? In legal terms, is that a fair *burden*? That subject will be addressed in detail in this book.

One last point. This book is timely, but for reasons that I was unaware when I began writing it. When Catholic Answers and I signed the contract for this book, the due month for the manuscript was September 2024. I feel slightly embarrassed to admit this, but I didn't realize the significance of this month. At a ceremony at Ave Maria University, my wife mentioned to a Franciscan priest that I was writing a book about the stigmata. He happily responded, "Oh, in honor of the 800th anniversary of St. Francis's reception of the stigmata?" My wife assumed that was why I was writing the book. Yet, when I began the book, I had no idea of that fact. But God knew, and that's what matters.

The Providence of God is exhilarating.

—John Francis Clark

September 14, 2024 | The 800th Anniversary of St. Francis's Reception of the Stigmata

ACKNOWLEDGEMENTS

Many people prayed for me and offered me help and encouragement as I wrote this book. There are several who deserve special thanks. My brother, Tim Clark, offered excellent logical and theological observations—as he so often does with my writing. Mary Beth Ellis proofread an early draft of the book and helped me provide more clarity to the reader. Jonathan Keenan, M.D., was exceedingly helpful by reviewing the book from a medical perspective. My wife, Lisa, offered me daily feedback as I read her new passages. I especially want to thank the talented and patient publishing team at Catholic Answers. Their exceptional counsel and brilliant insights made the final version of this book far better.

1

The First Stigmata: An Examination of Jesus' Wounds

Some years ago, my good friend Dr. Pasteau, the president of the Société de Saint-Luc of Catholic Doctors in France, was visiting the Vatican with several high dignitaries of the Church. He was explaining to them, following on my researches, how much we now know about the death of Jesus, about his terrible sufferings, and how he had died, suffering from cramps in all his muscles and from asphyxia. One of them, who was still Cardinal Pacelli, and who, along with the others, had gone pale with grief and compassion, answered him: "We did not know; nobody had ever told us that."

—Pierre Barbet[4]

On Ash Wednesday 2004, the eagerly-awaited movie *The Passion of the Christ* hit movie screens—but hit its viewers much harder. With ashen foreheads, Catholics across America cringed in their theater seats as they watched the portrayal of the intense whipping, beating, and stabbing of their Savior. Many in the audience openly wept as they peered at the screen and saw teams of Roman soldiers thrash Jesus' body with whips with metal hooks. The scene was violent, portraying the Roman soldiers covered in Jesus' blood, with only the physical exhaustion of the Roman soldiers finally slowing the assault. Most moviegoers had never seen any sort of brutality—real or imagined—like this. The two-hour depiction of Jesus' passion and death proved emotionally exhausting for the audience. A movie reviewer for the Evening Standard accounted that the cinematic "assault was so sustained and voyeuristic that most of the audience I saw the film with covered their eyes."[5] Another reviewer referred to it as a "primitive and pornographic bloodbath."[6]

As difficult as it was for the viewers to sit through these scenes, there is a reality that most audiences and reviewers missed: in comparison to the cinematic portrayal of the event, the actual crucifixion of Jesus was far worse. Some disbelievers may simply dismiss the account of Jesus' passion and crucifixion on the grounds that no human could survive such a physical assault. Yet, first-person accounts, ancient historians, and archaeology confirm that many thousands of men survived wanton scourging and lived—sometimes for days—on crosses before they succumbed to death. Even modern medical science confirms how that could occur. But the objectors are indeed correct on one essential point: crucifixion was almost indescribably violent and heartless. This is important to appreciate because within the sheer violence of the crucifixion lies much of the mystery behind the stigmata of the saints. Thus, in our quest to understand the *how* and *why* of the stigmata and stigmatists, we must begin by focusing on *the general nature and history of crucifixion itself* and, specifically, *the wounds of Christ.*

ROMAN CRUCIFIXION

Contemporary eyewitnesses, authors, and ancient and modern historians broadly confirm that crucifixion was a common practice before Constantine abolished it in the Roman Empire in the fourth century. In addition to the Romans, crucifixion was practiced by the Persians, Carthaginians, Babylonians, Egyptians, Greeks, Germanic peoples, Assyrians, British peoples, and others.[7] Considering its barbaric brutality, it is not observed lightly that crucifixion—in particular times and places—was a routine punishment. Several books have been written within the past few decades that have accumulated the historical findings illustrating widespread crucifixion, but our focus here is on *Roman* crucifixion—for that is what Jesus suffered. At first, that might seem overly exacting; after all, one might wonder, isn't there one basic method of crucifixion? But the answer is in the negative. As Martin Hengel notes in his book *Crucifixion*, "A particular problem is posed by the fact that the *form* of crucifixion varied considerably."[8] The Roman method proved particularly dehumanizing, unjust, and widespread.

A study of crucifixion is such an analysis of violence and savagery that it is easy to lose sight of a central aspect of crucifixion: its intentional degradation. Under some Roman emperors, crucifixion was a common punishment for slaves.[9] Cicero even refers to it as the *servitutis extremum summumque supplicium* (the highest and most extreme penalty for slaves).[10] In his oration known as *Against Verres*, Cicero expresses that crucifixion should only be used on slaves and never against a citizen: "It is a crime to bind a Roman citizen; to scourge him is a wickedness; to put him to death is almost parricide. What shall I say of crucifying him? So guilty an action cannot by any possibility be adequately expressed by any name bad enough for it."[11] Cicero's objection highlights a point:

crucifixion was broadly considered suitable for slaves. Crucifixion served a purpose beyond its ruthlessness: it confirmed that the crucified man or woman was—in fact—a slave. It was standard procedure for Roman authorities to make crucifixions as public as possible. It was not enough for the Romans to simply crucify slaves and leave their carcasses to serve as food for the birds in the middle of nowhere. Instead, the Romans used crucifixion as a socio-political statement. Historian Barry Strauss explains, "Roman authorities also favored the most crowded roads for crucifixions, in order to impress the maximum number of people."[12]

Not only was a *trial* unnecessary to crucify a slave, no *evidence* was necessary; in fact, no underlying *crime* was necessary. Horace provides the example of a slave who was crucified for tasting the soup of his master, but slaves were crucified for less.[13] Crucifixion was designed to illustrate ignobility; it was deemed the proper way to dispose of a slave. Simply put, slaves were treated as subhuman, and public crucifixion was designed to remind them—and all others who witnessed their deaths—of their sub-humanity.*

This anti-human view of slaves by the Romans is magnified by looking at the sheer volume of slaves who were crucified. The generational crucifixion of slaves was a reality alluded to around 205 B.C. in the play *Miles Gloriosus* written by Titus Maccius Plautus. The character Sceledrus states, "I know the cross will be my grave: that is where my ancestors are, my father, grandfathers, great-grandfathers, great-great-grandfathers."[14] That's an even more sobering

* It is worth noting that it was not only slaves who were crucified in the Roman Empire. Some freemen who were non-citizens were crucified. After all, the Gospel records that two thieves were crucified next to Jesus, but there is no indication that they were slaves. Nevertheless, the crucifixion of freemen was comparatively rare.

thought when considering how large the slave class was in the Roman Empire. Slavery was not the unhappy circumstance of only a handful of people. On the contrary, Strauss estimates the number of slaves in Italy at the time of Spartacus's uprising (73 B.C.) was between one and one-and-a-half million.[15] After that uprising, six thousand slaves were crucified, which was not an isolated event. Strauss notes that one of the mass crucifixions involved "2,000 rebels crucified in Judaea by the Roman official Quintilius Varus in 4 B.C."[16] But it was not just slave uprisings that led to crucifixions; Hengel notes that Caligula and Domitian "crucified imperial slaves . . . at their whim."[17] Seneca stated that slaves broadly lived "under the certain threat of crucifixion."[18]

As to the method of Roman crucifixion, the procedure generally occurred in three distinct stages: scourging at a pillar, the forced carrying of the cross, and nailing the victim to the cross where he would eventually die. Each stage consisted of a tortured madness in which human misery was viewed as entertaining theater.

Stage One: Scourging. Hengel writes, "In the Roman Empire . . . crucifixion was a punishment in which the caprice and sadism of the executioners were given full rein."[19] That is no overstatement, especially considering that the process of scourging was given to those men who most enjoyed scourging others in the first place. In his book describing his experiences in a Nazi concentration camp, *Man's Search For Meaning*, Viktor Frankl noted, "When the SS took a dislike to a person, there was always some special man in their ranks known to have a passion for, and to be highly specialized in, sadistic torture, to whom the unfortunate prisoner was sent."[20] The same basic process played out in the Roman scourging process; that is, the Roman authorities sought out the most sadistic men to perform vicious fantasies known only to men who get their marching orders from demons.[21]

The word "scourging" comes to us in English from the medieval French word *escorgier*, which means "to whip."[22] But the word fails to capture its innate ferocity. The victim's wrists were tied to a post so that he could not defend himself against the weapons of torture, and then the beating commenced. In his book The *Wars of The Jews*, Jewish historian Flavius Josephus (A.D. 37–100) writes about the infliction of "stripes" before crucifixion, recounting that a woman was "torn to pieces with the stripes."[23] This was standard by design. One of the most popular devices used to scourge victims was the "scorpion." This was a multi-thronged leather whip with affixed bone or metal. It was designed to hack into flesh and tear off the flesh to the bone. Numerous writers in antiquity affirm this fact, including Josephus, who wrote about the scourging of a man who "was whipped till his bones were laid bare."[24]

Scourging was often conducted in such a way as to inflict the absolute maximum possible amount of pain without killing the victim; however, many victims of scourging died in the process. One researcher notes that "Livy, Suetonius, and Josephus all report cases of flagellation in which the lictors went too far, and their victims died while still bound to the post."[25] Nevertheless, the Romans often took it upon themselves to nail the scourged, dead bodies to crosses for public display. There were also instances in which the scourgers lost all interest in keeping their victims alive; with demonic ferocity, the soldiers simply beat them to death. And beyond death. The historian Eusebius gives us the account of eyewitnesses at the scene when a group of St. Polycarp's contemporaries were scourged to death: "For they say that the bystanders were struck with amazement when they saw them lacerated with scourges even to the innermost veins and arteries, so that the hidden inward parts of the body, both their bowels and their members, were exposed to view; and then laid upon sea-shells and certain pointed spits, and subjected to every species of punishment and of torture, and finally thrown as food to wild beasts."[26]

Stage Two: Carrying the Cross. For those who did survive the initial scourging—and the vast majority seem to have done so—the next step was forcing the victim to carry the wood of the cross to the designated place of death. For our purposes here, there is no need to go into great detail regarding this process other than pointing out the following: carrying the wood of the cross to the place of death deliberately compounded the suffering already inflicted by the scourging.[27] The shoulders, already ripped open by scourging, then had to endure carrying a massive piece of wood. This weight deeply compounded the pain of the open shoulder wound. The scourged shoulder would have been inexpressibly painful with even the slightest touch; the pain of putting a hundred pounds on that wound—and feeling it boring an even deeper wound—is unimaginable. It is grimly telling that the Roman philosopher Seneca, in observing the swelling of the crucified with "ugly weals on shoulders," considered suicide as a preferable option to crucifixion.[28]

*Stage Three: Nailing to the Cross.** After recounting the pro-

* Perhaps in an effort to defeat the integrity of the New Testament, some modern writers, historians, and even some anti-Catholic Christians have sought to illustrate that the Romans used a pole—rather than a cross—for crucifixion. But it was most certainly a cross. Confirmation of that fact is evidenced by Scripture, including each of the Gospels. As Woodrow Michael Kroll points out, "In the New Testament, the word "cross" (Greek: σταυρός; *stauros*) occurs twenty-seven times in twenty-seven verses." That it was a cross is further evidenced by the early Church fathers. Beyond that, the fact that the Romans routinely used crosses for crucifixion is evidenced by contemporary non-Christian historians such as Flavius Josephus.

cess of scourging and carrying the cross, it is striking that some ancient writers consider this the most violent stage of Roman crucifixion. Though victims were sometimes tied to their crosses, they were typically nailed to the cross. In what seems to have been deemed a particular form of cruelty, "some were crucified upside down."[29] But they were not left to die alone. As Barbet notes, a Roman guard remained—in part—to ensure that the crucified man was not rescued by friends or family by the dead of night.[30] But some guards occupied their time in sadism. Some of the crucified continued to be beaten and jeered on the cross as they approached their deaths. It also occurred that visiting wives, children, and friends of the crucified had their throats slit as the crucified men watched helplessly from their crosses. (This might shed new light on the reluctance of the apostles to visit Jesus on the cross and provide an increased appreciation of Mary, Mary Magdalene, and John the apostle who stood at the foot of the cross.) One of the most significant variables was how long it took for the victim to die: some died quickly; others survived for days. Typically, the Romans allowed, by design, birds and wild animals to eat the crucified carcasses for food; however, the Romans did sometimes allow families to claim the bodies.

THE UNIQUE WOUNDS OF JESUS

Jesus bore some injuries in common with most others who endured Roman crucifixion, but he also had unique wounds. To understand subsequent cases of stigmata, we must first grasp Jesus' suffering and wounds—which we might call the first stigmata. To determine the extent and particular nature of Jesus' injuries, it would be reasonable to first turn to Scripture. The difficulty, however, is that the scriptures are not very detailed. For instance, regarding the hyper-violent and bloodthirsty scourging of Jesus at the pillar, the Gospel of Matthew simply states, "Then he released for them Barab'bas, and having scourged Jesus, delivered him to be crucified" (Matt. 27:26). Regarding the Crucifixion, Mark's Gospel simply states, "And they crucified him" (Mark 15:24). Luke's Gospel gives more attention to the burial of Jesus than to the specifics of his injuries. We may reasonably ask, *Why is there such a lack of details?* The answer given by Barbet, is simple. He writes, "The Evangelists certainly had no need to be more explicit. For the Christians who had listened to the apostolic teaching, and who later on read the four Gospels, these two words, 'scourging, crucifixion,' were all too full of meaning; they had firsthand experience, and had seen scourgings and crucifixions; they knew what the words meant."[31]

As will be shown later in this chapter, scourging and crucifixion continued for three centuries after Jesus' death and resurrection; thus, the early Christians were presented with physical reminders of Jesus' torment until the time of Constantine—who abolished crucifixion in the Roman Empire. Subsequent ages, however, increasingly lost sight—and understanding—of these terms. Simply, relying on Scripture alone does not provide us enough insight in the third millennia after Christ. Thus, we need to turn to more sources. Regarding crucifixion generally, we have already referenced ancient historians and archaeological findings for details. Moving on, we will examine several more sources for clues and explanations—notably, the writings of the Church Fathers, approved private revelation, and the Shroud of Turin. We can also touch upon the advantage of the advances in science and medicine. In some respects, from the perspective of modern medicine, we now know more about Jesus' wounds and sufferings than ever before. The most logical way to proceed in an understanding of the first stigmata—the stigmata of Jesus—is to look at them from a chronological perspective, beginning with the events of Holy Thursday and culminating with the Resurrection.

THURSDAY NIGHT/FRIDAY PRE-DAWN

The Sweating of Blood. After the institution of the Eucharist at the Last Supper, and just before his arrest, Jesus went to the Mount of Olives to pray. The Gospel of Luke informs us, "And being in an agony he prayed more earnestly; and his sweat became like great drops of blood falling down upon the ground" (22:44). Until recently, sweating blood was considered a physical impossibility. Many skeptics have denied the episode entirely. Even many devout Christians over the centuries have sought to explain Luke's passage as a mere metaphor. For instance, Aquinas cites the late Father of the Church, Theophylact, who opined, "Or this is *proverbially* said of one who has sweated intensely, that he sweated blood; the Evangelist then wishing to shew that he was moistened with large drops of sweat, takes drops of blood for an example"[32] (emphasis added).

Other Christians have regarded it as a miraculous occurrence. In his commentary on that verse, St. Bede writes that "it is contrary to nature to sweat blood."[33] Meanwhile, many others, such as Francisco Suarez and St. Augustine, accept this event as natural.[34] At the same time, Augustine gives a mystical explanation *why* Jesus sweat blood: "Our Lord praying with a bloody sweat represented the martyrdoms which should flow from his whole body, which is the Church."[35]

Though the claim of sweating blood has often been doubted for over two millennia, it should be noted that sweating blood was a phenomenon that occurred in others as well during those times—and even prior. In his treatise, *The History of Animals*, Aristotle even stated that when "animals fall sick . . . the blood then turns into . . . a liquid so thin that it at times has been known to exude through the pores like sweat."[36] Leonardo da Vinci referenced a soldier who sweat blood before battle.[37] Fr. Andrew Breen also noted several other cases in Europe: one woman under immense fear of being sexually assaulted, a man condemned to death in Germany, and another condemned man in France.[38] The common denominator was intense anxiety. When Breen's book was published in 1908, such claims may have been doubted. But that brings us to the present day, which provides ample new evidence and casts aside all reasonable doubt about the reality that one can sweat blood.

In July 2009, *The Indian Journal of Dermatology* issued a report confirming sweating blood. The study noted a patient who had repeatedly sweat blood, speculated to be the result of "continuous mental stress for two years due to family feud."[39] They mentioned others, including "six cases in men condemned to execution, a case occurring during the London blitz, a case involving fear of being raped, a case of fear of a storm while sailing."[40] The physicians conclude, "Acute fear and intense mental contemplation are the most frequent causes."[41] Similar case studies were reported in the past two decades including articles in *Blood*, the official magazine of *The American Society of Hematology* (2013),[42] and DermNet (2021). Moreover, though the condition is exceedingly rare, cases continue to surface. In 2023, an article in *Dermatology Reports* confirmed that a young girl was afflicted with sweating blood, the cause of which was deemed to be "separation anxiety disorder during COVID-19 quarantine."[43]

Though it took nineteen centuries to provide, we now have firsthand medical confirmation for the naturalness—

albeit rarity—of the malady of sweating blood. We also have a name for it: *hematohidrosis*. Further, we have a great insight into its cause: extreme emotional distress. St. Luke, a physician by trade, noted the reality and confirmed the cause of hematohidrosis nineteen centuries ago.

Why take pains to point out that sweating blood is a *natural* occurrence rather than a *miraculous* one? Because to appreciate the passion and death of Jesus more fully, it is essential to understand that Jesus did not simply *appear* to suffer; Jesus actually suffered and died on the cross. Though miracles indeed occurred during his passion, there can be no doubt that Jesus—who took on human nature to save us from our sins—suffered in his humanity more than anyone before or since.

The Wounds of Jesus' Arrest and Trials. After Jesus was comforted by an angel, he was arrested by a group of angry soldiers and archers directed by Judas. The Gospel accounts do not provide much detail about his arrest, but we can assume violence, especially considering the incident of Peter cutting off the ear of Malchus. In the writings detailing her visions, Bl. Anne Catherine Emmerich provides specific details:

> The archers, who now proceeded to pinion Jesus with the greatest brutality . . . They tied his hands as tightly as possible with hard new cords, fastening the right-hand wrist under the left elbow, and the left-hand wrist under the right elbow. They encircled his waist with a species of belt studded with iron points, and to this collar were appended two leathern straps, which were crossed over his chest like a stole and fastened to the belt. They then fastened four ropes to different parts of the belt, and by means of these ropes dragged our Blessed Lord from side to side in the most cruel manner . . .

> They led him along the roughest road they could select, over the sharpest stones, and through the thickest mire; they pulled the cords as tightly as possible; they struck him with knotted cords, as a butcher would strike the beast he is about to slaughter.[44]

Emmerich goes on to describe that Jesus was beaten so hard that he was knocked off a bridge before being retrieved. She continues,

> It was not quite midnight when I saw the four archers inhumanly dragging Jesus over a narrow path, which was choked up with stones, fragments of rock, thistles, and thorns, on the opposite shore of the Cedron. The six brutal Pharisees walked as close to our Lord as they could, struck him constantly with thick pointed sticks, and . . . his bare and bleeding feet were torn by the stones and briars.[45]

Thus, Jesus suffered immensely even before his appearance at his trial—the most famous and infamous show trial in history. The illegal proceedings began by taking Jesus to the former high priest Annas.[46] The Gospel of John tells us that an officer struck Jesus during this meeting (18:23). After Annas questioned Jesus, he was taken to the Sanhedrin to face the high priest, Cai'aphas, where he was questioned, mocked, and beaten. Matthew recounts, "Then they spat in his face, and struck him; and some slapped him" (26:67). Mark states that "the guards received him with blows" (14:65). Luke's Gospel clarifies that Jesus was repeatedly assaulted while blindfolded.

How many people were beating Jesus at the show trial? By rule, there had to be at least twenty-three members of the Sanhedrin present since that was roughly the number required to form a quorum.[47] But Anne Catherine Emmerich puts the number of Sanhedrin members at seventy, not to mention others, including "false witnesses."[48] Judging by their illegal actions at the trial, it is possible that many of these men hit or slapped Jesus, even taking repeated turns at Jesus. After the first trial, Jesus was thrown into prison, where he likely suffered even more physical abuse. Christians often think of Jesus' passion beginning on Friday with the scourging at the pillar. But it is clear that, by the time the sun rose on Friday, Jesus had already undergone immense suffering throughout his body.

GOOD FRIDAY

The Crowning with Thorns. We have already addressed the Roman process of scourging in detail, to which Jesus was subject, but there was an added brutality against Jesus that was unique: the crowning with thorns. To mock the idea that Jesus was the King of the Jews, the torturers of Jesus took it upon themselves to inflict this painful and bloody mockery. The Gospel of Matthew describes, "plaiting a crown of thorns they put it on his head." (27:29)

The fact that Jesus endured crowning with thorns is front and center in Catholic devotion to the passion of Jesus, but many Catholics may not be aware that the crown of thorns still exists and is currently held in France. Two millennia after the Passion, the crown of thorns was back in the news because of the fire in Notre Dame, in which a priest heroically rushed in to save the precious relic. Though some doubt that this is the actual crown, it should be noted that its existence has been referenced at least as far back as the year 409 by St. Paulinus of Nola (354–431) and confirmed by others such as Cassiodorus in 570 and St. Gregory of Tours in 587.[49] How it came to be at Notre Dame has a fascinating history, but it seems to have been accounted for during sixteen centuries.[50] If the question remains about the four centuries before Paulinus, we might simply point out that Christianity was a capital crime in the Roman Empire until the fourth century under Constantine—thus, Christians could not prudently advertise their possession of relics.

When we look at the typical crown of a king or queen, we can see that only a tiny part of the crown touches the head. The circumference of the crown rests *around* the head but does not touch the rest of the scalp. At first glance, the surviving crown in Notre Dame seems to share that characteristic. Thus, when we read Matthew, we might naturally imagine that the thorns only pressed into the area around the top of Jesus' head. Yet, we must remember that thorns have been broken off the central portion of the crown; after all, over the centuries, various churches and persons have claimed to own and venerate individual thorns. But Barbet claims that the thorns of our Lord's crown covered his head on Good Friday. Though the crown was formed into a circular ring, the thorns were woven into a cap to pierce the entire top of his head. (The plant used to form the crown is known to botany as *Ziziphus spina-christi*, or in more layman's terms, Christ's thorn jujube.[51] When looking at that plant, it is easy to see how the soldiers could quickly form a crown.)

In his *Sermon on Good Friday*, the Dominican priest St. Vincent Ferrer (1350–1419) explains, "Shaping a crown of marine [*marinis*] thorns, which have sharper and longer spines than other thorns, they pressed it on his head, cruelly wounding it in seventy-two places. It was shaped like a cap [*ad modum pilei*] so that wherever it contacted the head, the spines penetrated to the skull."[52] St. Bridget of Sweden's apparitions confirm this number of seventy-two.

Of all the parts of the body, head wounds are the most potentially bloody because of the collection of veins that reside in the head. As the University of Utah Health states, "Your scalp can bleed profusely from even a minor cut."[53] The crown of thorns was no minor cut. Instead, the crown produced seventy-two deep punctures to the head, which caused Jesus' face to be drenched in blood and his hair to be dripping with blood. By this point, Jesus' face would have been nearly unrecognizable to any but his closest friends and his mother. It is no wonder that the Stations of the Cross remember particularly the bloodied face of Jesus under the guise of tender ministrations offered by St. Veronica.

The Piercing of His Side and Heart. Matthew, Mark, and Luke's Gospels do not mention this particular posthumous event, but John's Gospel describes it in detail. The Roman soldiers, following the law, were given the job to ensure that all three crucified men were positively dead before their bodies could be delivered to their families. The soldiers broke the legs of the crucified men on both sides of Jesus; however, "when they came to Jesus and saw that he was already dead, they did not break his legs. But one of the soldiers pierced his side with a spear, and at once there came out blood and water" (19:33–34). The very next verse highlights the extreme importance of this incident: "He who saw it has borne witness—his testimony is true, and he knows that he tells the truth—that you also may believe" (19:35).[54]

In this act of stabbing his side, the soldier intentionally also pierced Jesus' heart. How do we know? Though the Gospel of John does not explicitly tell us that Jesus' heart was punctured, we can infer it from his description of blood and water gushing forth. Barbet explains how we know and also how we know that the soldier pierced Jesus' right side. The soldier needed to ensure that Jesus was dead, but the mere act of stabbing his side would not have definitively induced or confirmed death; as we have seen, Jesus had already suffered far worse and survived. Thus, the intention of the soldier was not merely to pierce Jesus' side but to drive the spear through his side, past his ribs, and puncture his heart. Barbet explains that this technique of fatally driving a spear into the right side of the opponent's heart was standard practice for Roman soldiers. Barbet explains,

> This blow at the heart from the right was always mortal, and must have become classical and have been taught in the fencing-schools of the Roman armies. . . . Blows into the intercostal spaces on the right edge of the breastbone do not allow of recovery, because they open up the very thin wall of the right auricle. And this is still true today, even when a surgeon can intervene quickly.[55]

Barbet explains that although people often consider the heart to occupy only the left side of the chest, sections of the heart also occupy the right: "Now, *and this is the important side of the question*, the part of the heart which extends to the right of the breastbone *is the right auricle*. And this auricle, which is prolonged upwards by the superior vena cava, and downwards by the inferior vena cava, is *in a corpse always filled with liquid blood*."[56] The fact that John testifies to water and blood provides further medical confirmation. Barbet explains that when a heart is punctured, pericardial fluid—which contains water—pours out. In sum, modern medicine evidences the process that John described.

There is one final point here that underscores John's eyewitness testimony about the heart wound. After his resurrection, Jesus—now with a glorified body—had been seen by some of the apostles; however, Thomas the apostle had not seen him. Thomas doubted their accounts of seeing Jesus and was adamant in his doubt. Thomas said, "Unless I see in his hands the print of the nails, and place my finger in the mark of the nails, and place my hand in his side, I will not believe" (John 20:25). Note that Thomas does not say "in the mark of his side," but rather "in his side." Eight days after the Resurrection, when the apostles were gathered together, Jesus passed through the closed doors and stood before Thomas. Jesus invites Thomas to inspect his wounds: "Put your finger here, and see my hands; and put out your hand, and place it in my side; do not be faithless, but believing" (John 20:27). Consider that Jesus offers Thomas to put only a finger on his hand wounds but his entire hand in his side. The Gospel does not precisely tell us, but it is inferred that Jesus is inviting Thomas to feel the wound in his Sacred Heart.

When we discuss the major wounds Jesus received in his passion and death, it is essential to highlight that the Shroud of Turin serves as a detailed confirmation of the wounds described in this chapter.

THE GLORIOUS SCANDAL OF THE CROSS

In the following chapters, we will examine the lives and wonders of those men and women who miraculously bore the wounds of Jesus. But it is essential to understand that many early Christians bore wounds like those of Jesus. But their wounds were not produced mystically; instead, they were inflicted upon them by Roman leaders driven mad in an effort to eliminate Christianity. After the crucifixion of Jesus, the Roman governments proceeded to go on a crucifixion spree. And as we are about to see, the heroic response of the martyrs would inspire the world.

As we discussed earlier in this chapter, crucifixion was a common punishment for slaves; in fact, to crucify a man was meant to re-affirm his status as a slave. As Hengel writes, "Death on the cross was the penalty for slaves, as everyone knew; as such it symbolized extreme humiliation, shame and torture."[57] Thus, the crucifixion of Jesus was not merely about punishing, mocking, and insulting Jesus. It was not merely to treat him as a subhuman slave. Beyond all that, his crucifixion was meant to send a warning to his followers: if you persist in Christianity, you will experience the same brutal, vile, and slavish fate. Of course, that warning was promptly, defiantly, and widely ignored. Men, women, and children practiced Christianity across the empire, and the empire struck back. The Romans were true to their threat.

Though many Christians think of being thrown to the lions as the standard method of execution, the *Roman Martyrology* recounts that in the infancy of the Church, crucifixion was common. Moreover, the Romans did not discriminate in deciding those who received such execution. Both old and young, both clergy and laity, both men and women—all groups were subject to death on a cross. The apostle Philip was crucified and stoned to death as he hung on the cross. St. Faustus suffered a similar fate and, after having the audacity to survive for five days on the cross, he was shot with arrows until he died. Under the tyranny of Diocletian, St. Agricola was crucified "with many nails."[58] Nero crucified rows of Christians and burned their bodies as human torches. St. Appolinus was crucified. Newlyweds Timothy and Maura were crucified together after a series of tortures that included blinding.

The martyrology speaks of many others: "At Ægæa, in Cilicia, the holy martyrs Claudius, Asterius, and Neon, brothers, who were accused of being Christians by their step-mother, under the emperor Diocletian, and the governor Lysias, and after enduring bitter torments, were fastened to a cross, and thus conquered and triumphed with Christ."[59] Under Diocletian's terrorizing rule, in the year 287, Arabian twin brothers and physicians Cosmas and Damian underwent crucifixion, but their persecutors seemed to grow tired of waiting for them to die—eventually beheading them, along with their three brothers.[60] The list goes on. Thus, when we speak about those saints who bore the stigmata—the wounds of Christ—it is clear that some early Christians bore remarkably similar wounds as a result of their own crucifixions. In that respect, the first saint to bear the stigmata was indeed St. Dismas, the good thief who was crucified alongside Jesus—and canonized by Jesus while he hung on his cross.

The Romans had intended the cross to be a fearful scandal—a stumbling block—to following Christ, but the exact opposite occurred. The cross became a symbol of everlasting triumph. St. Paul says as much: "For Jews demand signs and Greeks seek wisdom, but we preach Christ crucified, a stumbling block to Jews and folly to Gentiles, but to those who are called, both Jews and Greeks, Christ the power of God and the wisdom of God. For the foolishness of God is wiser than men, and the weakness of God is stronger than men" (1 Cor. 1:22–25). The idea of someone making *the sign of the cross* would have seemed extraordinarily bizarre to everyone in the Roman Empire before the Crucifixion. From the perspective of the Romans, the cross was considered beneath the dignity of Roman citizens—even if they were terrible criminals.

But Christians held the cross in such magnificent esteem that they did not even consider themselves worthy of the cross. Of the crucified martyrs, the most notable was St. Peter, the first pope. Tradition holds that Peter made it clear to his persecutors that he was not worthy to die in the same manner as his Savior; thus, he insisted on being crucified upside down. Peter and these early crucified martyrs realized the profound dignity of suffering like Christ, for their bodies embodied the suffering that their Savior underwent. They were, in a profound sense, sharing in his passion.

If the thought of a Christian uniting his suffering with Jesus seems odd, consider our English word "compassion." The word comes to English from the Latin and French words *com* ("together") plus *patir* ("to suffer"). Thus, *compassion* means "to suffer together," and it is broadly considered to be a noble virtue. What mother, seeing her child suffer, has not wished that she could take on some of her child's pain—to *suffer with* and alleviate the pain in some way? And this brings us to the role of Mary in the Passion. By divine design, no human nor angel will ever be as close to God as Mary, the Mother of God. As much as the stigmatists suffered from physical pain—and as we are about to see, they suffered immense physical pain—it stands to reason that Mary suffered more than any of them because of her closeness with her Son. Although she may not have sustained a stigmatic pain of the body, she undoubtedly suffered from mental and emotional anguish.

There are various prayerful and penitential ways to honor Jesus' passion and death. For instance, we Catholics pray the Sorrowful Mysteries, during which we ponder the suffering and crucifixion Jesus endured for us. But we can also honor Jesus' suffering by uniting it with our own. This point warrants an important point: though we Catholics speak about the value of suffering, we do not generally go around *searching* for ways to suffer. In a fallen world, suffering finds us, just as it finds the rest of humanity. But when we willingly accept our suffering and unite it with Jesus' passion, we see the good that can be gained through suffering. As we are about to examine, some suffer more than others.

This chapter has sought to examine the wounds of Jesus' passion and death because without having a solid knowledge of these, the wounds of the stigmatists would be confusing and inexplicable. Going forward, we will see that each of the significant wounds that Jesus suffered was experienced, in some measure, by one or more stigmatists—including, as we will see, heart stigmata. Though the stigmata vary from person to person, the common denominator is intense pain. As Fr. Charles M. Carty explains in *The Stigmata and Modern Science,* "The vocation of the stigmatists is to suffer a share of the passion of Christ—which exceeds all earthly sufferings."[61] As we will see, that is an accurate description.

2

A REFLECTION OF CHRIST: THE MIRACLE OF ST. FRANCIS

> For St. Francis of Assisi had a charism perhaps more intense than that given to any other man since the apostles; he and his first followers truly believed that they could live out their lives almost like angels—as indeed they could, so long as St. Francis was with them.
>
> —Warren H. Carroll[62]

There is a saying among Catholic theologians that a hundred questions do not add up to a single doubt. That is, when a Catholic asks sincere questions about his faith—even those involving doctrinal matters—the questions do not, per se, signify a lack of belief. Often, it is quite the contrary: for the person trying to deeply understand, his questions signify a magnificent process called *wonder.* On the subject of wonder, Aquinas writes, "Wonder gives pleasure, not because it implies ignorance, but in so far as it includes the desire of learning the cause, and in so far as the wonderer learns something new, i.e., that the cause is other than he had thought it to be."[63]

Of course, wonder not only helps us learn something new; it leads to more wonder. Just as Aristotle deemed wonder to be the beginning of philosophy, it is also the beginning of theology, i.e., the scrutiny of divine things. Though the Catholic theology student—as well as the master—might ask a million different questions in a myriad of ways, he is essentially asking the same one: *who is God?* The very question draws us closer to him; in that respect, theological wonder is less a path than a ladder. These same principles apply to the stigmata. What do the stigmata tell us about God? How can the stigmata help us answer the question, *who is God?*

One may firmly believe in the mysterious reality of the stigmata yet ask legitimate questions. *Why did twelve hundred years pass between our Lord's passion and the stigmata of St. Francis? Why not sooner? Why were there no stigmatists for twelve centuries and then so many after that? For that matter, why Francis in the first place? Why not St. Augustine or St. Philomena or St. John the Beloved? Did Francis have different virtues than the other saints who preceded him? If so, what were they?*

At the outset, we might note that these questions parallel those that could be asked about Marian apparitions. Fifteen centuries elapsed between Our Lady's assumption and her apparition at Guadalupe in 1531. Yet, between 1830 and 1917, Mary appeared no fewer than five times—and three times in France alone. Why so many times, so suddenly? And why France, as opposed to Italy, Spain, or anywhere else? We might further note a parallel to the life of Jesus, who lived a private life for thirty years and then worked a great series of public miracles after his miracle at Cana. In the final analysis, these questions remain wondrous mysteries. Yet, perhaps the life of Francis can give us an insight into all of these questions.

THE IMITATION OF CHRIST

It is a curious fact that modern men and women, even anti-Catholics, have an affection for Francis. His love for the poor, his compassion for the marginalized, his message of peace, his affection for animals, and his respect for the earth—these virtues have captivated audiences for centuries. The modern audience, however, tends to leave God out of the Francis equation. But to tell the story of Francis without God is to misunderstand him utterly. Without God, his talk of Brother Sun and Sister Moon is tragically misunderstood as pantheist environmentalism; his call for poverty is misinterpreted as Marxist socialism; his greeting of peace is misplaced as pacifism. Without exception, Francis's good works were motivated by the love of God and his powerful desire to imitate Christ; as we will see, this is a vital thing for us to understand regarding the stigmata.

Every practicing Catholic realizes—in some sense and degree—that he is called to imitate Christ; yet, it has been argued that no man since Apostolic times has imitated Christ more perfectly than Francis of Assisi.[64] The barefoot friar was a walking treatise on virtues. His name is nearly synonymous with the virtue of poverty, but he was no less an exemplar of faith, hope, charity, humility, peace, chastity, compassion, and obedience. And even beyond that, his virtues seem contagious: nearly all those around him seemed to become better men and women for the association—and thousands of people wanted to be around him. Many men dropped everything to follow him. Francis healed lepers, ardently prayed at great length in private, was assisted by angels, called for the repentance of sinners, gathered disciples, worked miracles, and cast out demons—all in the name of Jesus.

It might otherwise be easy to dismiss many of the wondrous accounts and miracles of Francis's life, except that crowds of people witnessed so many of these events. It speaks volumes that Francis was canonized only twenty-two months after his death. In his bull of canonization, Pope Gregory IX writes that "we are fully convinced by reliable witnesses of the many brilliant miracles" involving Francis.[65] Such witnesses were easy to find; by the end of his life, Francis was one of the most well-known people on earth—and perhaps the most loved person on earth. Beyond those eyewitnesses, we have contemporary written biographies of Francis by Thomas of Celano and St. Bonaventure.

Francis's story begins in 1181, when he was born into a wealthy merchant family of Assisi. His father was Italian and his mother was French—a fact that likely influenced his name.[66] Bonaventure notes that, although the young Francis was happy to party lavishly with friends, he had "a certain innate and natural love of the poor of Christ."[67] In his early twenties, Francis became involved in a conflict between the towns of Assisi and Perugia, and was captured and held as a prisoner-of-war for a year. During his captivity, he became so ill that he was given the anointing of the sick. After his release, Francis had a powerful dream, which he interpreted as being God's will that he become a soldier. A later dream confirmed that he was meant not to be a military soldier but a soldier for Christ.

While he waited for a more precise message, Francis became convinced that he must be poor. While riding his horse one morning, Francis came across a leper. At first, Francis was repulsed, but repulsion was quickly overcome with compassion. He turned back, dismounted, hugged the leper, kissed the leper's hand, and then put money in his hand. After turning his back to the leper to remount his horse, Francis turned around, only to discover that the leper had vanished. Francis had received a sign from God and now knew how to devote his life.[68]

Francis was cheerful and fearless in accepting his cross and following Jesus—a reality well-illustrated in Francis's life among the lepers. Lest we forget in our modern age, leprosy prior to the discovery of antibiotics of modern times was, in effect, a death sentence. Because others were terrified of contracting the disease by contagious contact, lepers were sent to colonies, or *leprosaria*, to not only wither and die in agony, but to die lonely. As an article in *Medical Daily* chillingly describes, "Throughout most of history, if you had leprosy, you were doomed to a life of isolation—and could expect to never hold, or even see, your children or family members ever again."[69]

Yet, inspired by how Jesus touched and healed lepers, Francis chose to live among them. Bonaventure writes, "And inasmuch as heretofore he had greatly abhorred the company of lepers, and could not endure even the distant sight of them, now—for the love of Christ crucified, who, according to the Prophet's words, was despised as a leper—he, in contempt of himself, sought out and served lepers with great humility and piety, and aided them in all their necessities. For he often visited them in their houses, giving them bountiful alms, and with affectionate compassion he would kiss their hands and their faces."[70] Further, it was common knowledge that God had given Francis the power to work miracles and cure some of the lepers.

Francis was not only able save lives through healing miracles, but he also proved uniquely able to quell violence; further, he was insightful enough to recognize the genesis of much violence: the instigation of demons. As Francis and his fellow monks came up the walled city of Arezzo, the city was besieged by violence among its citizens. So Francis instructed Brother Sylvester to cast out these demons who were inciting violence in the city. Sylvester exorcised them, shouting: "In the Name of Almighty God, and by the command of his servant Francis, I bid you all, infernal demons, to depart far from hence."[71] Bonaventure notes, "No sooner had he spoken than the tumult in the city was appeased."[72]

This was not the only encounter between the devils and Francis. The devils seemed acutely aware of Francis's holiness, so they conspired on many occasions to tempt and trick him. Francis would routinely cast himself into the snow to fight temptations of the flesh, so the devil said to him, "There is no sinner in the world, who, if he be converted, shall not obtain pardon of God. But he who shall destroy himself by excessive penance shall obtain no mercy for all eternity."[73] It is interesting here that the devil tempts Francis against avoiding temptation. The devil followed with a temptation against chastity, and Francis responded again by casting himself into the snow. After that incident, God guarded Francis from having temptations against chastity ever again.[74]

Francis's love of chastity was also inspired by his devotion to the Blessed Virgin Mary. During his early period of spiritual discernment, Francis prayed in an old Assisi church called *St. Mary of the Portiuncula*, or *Our Lady of the Angels*. The church had been abandoned and was falling apart, but Francis—inspired by an "exceeding love" of "the mother of Christ"—determined to repair it.[75] "This place was loved by the holy man above all places in the world, for here, in great humility, he began his spiritual life; here he grew in virtue; here he attained his happy and perfect end; and this, at the hour of his death, he commended to his brethren as a spot most dear to the Blessed Virgin." Mary—who had knelt under the foot of Jesus' cross after one apostle had betrayed Jesus and ten apostles were nowhere to be found—would be a constant companion and guide for Francis from his first visit to this little church through the hour of his earthly death. Through Mary's advocacy and intercession, Francis was sure that he was called to begin an order, but that could not be accomplished without papal approval.

Thus, in his late twenties, Francis and some followers approached Pope Innocent III to request his approval to start an officially recognized order. The pontiff initially rejected Francis's request, deeming his penitential and austere way of life impossible to follow. Francis accepted the pope's decision in the practice of the virtue of obedience. Bonaventure notes Francis's love of that virtue as well, "For he declared that, so abundant is the fruit of holy obedience, that to those who place their neck beneath its yoke, no place and no time shall be without its profit."[76] Nevertheless, after a dream in which Innocent saw Francis supporting the Lateran Basilica on his shoulders, the pope wholeheartedly changed his mind. Bonaventure notes that Pope Innocent "was filled with a great and special devotion and love for" Francis and approved of his new order in 1209.[77] In humility, Francis called his order the "Order of Friars Minor."[78] From there, the order became world-famous during Francis's lifetime.

For purposes of this book's thesis, we must now focus on two essential aspects of Francis: his devotion to the Eucharist and his devotion to the passion of Christ. (As we will see, these twin devotions are common denominators among the stigmatists.)

Francis's desire to imitate Christ was born of a profound love of Christ, evidenced in his love and adoration for the Eucharist in word and deed. His biographers note that Francis's love and adoration for the Eucharist was a continual theme in his exhortations.[79] In an admonition, Francis writes, "He shows himself to us in this sacred bread just as he once appeared to his apostles in real flesh. With their own eyes they saw only his flesh, but they believed that he was God, because they contemplated him with the eyes of the spirit. We, too, with our own eyes, see only bread and wine, but we must see further and firmly believe that this is his most holy Body and Blood, living and true."[80] Francis goes on to assure us that the real presence of Jesus in the Eucharist is the manifestation of his promise: "Behold I am with you all days, even to the consummation of the world" (Matt. 28:20).[81] In his *Letter to All Clerics*, Francis also warned priests against receiving the Eucharist "unworthily" and administering the Eucharist to "all-comers without distinction."[82]

When examining Francis's devotion to the passion of Christ, we must begin by looking at an incident that occurred in his twenties that would forever affect Francis's life. When praying in solitude, Jesus appeared to Francis. Bonaventure describes,

> Jesus Christ appeared to him under the form of a crucifix, at which sight his whole soul seemed to melt away; and so deeply was the memory of Christ's passion impressed on his heart, that it pierced even to the marrow of his bones. *From that hour, whenever he thought upon the passion of Christ, he could scarcely restrain his tears and sighs*; for he then understood (as he made known to some of his familiar friends not long before his death) that these words of the Gospel were addressed to him: "If thou wilt come after me, deny thyself, and take up thy cross and follow me."[83]

Another time, Francis was seen wandering and weeping around the chapel of the Portiuncula when a man approached Francis and asked him why he was in overwhelming sadness. Francis responded, "I am weeping over the sufferings of my Lord Jesus Christ, and I am not ashamed to wander around the world and weep over them." The man responded in kind and began weeping alongside Francis. [84] This early event in the two-decade span of Francis's ministry foretold that his devotion to the Passion would lead others to a similar devotion. Such devotion did Francis have to the cross that he forbade his friars to ever step upon any branches or hay that lay in a cruciform pattern.[85] We also see this particular piety in Francis's writings, especially in his institution of an *Office of the Passion of the Lord*, which was meant to be prayed not only during Holy Week, but throughout the year.[86] Fr. Solanus Benfatti also points to a rather obvious indication of Francis's deep devotion to the passion and death of Jesus: "Francis adopted the *tau* cross even as his own signature."[87]

Thus, we can see that Francis had powerful and unwavering devotion to the passion of Jesus, and to the Eucharist. As Franciscan father Pascal Robinson writes, "Because St. Francis loved Jesus and his eucharistic passion, ardently, enthusiastically, almost desperately—to borrow Bossuet's adjectives—his sympathy extended to every creature that suffered or rejoiced."[88] These devotions, coupled with an ardent desire to imitate Christ, would change his life and the world because a perfect imitation of Christ would involve a reflection of our Lord's life and his death.

FRANCIS RECEIVES THE STIGMATA

In the Italian region of Tuscany stands a mountain called La Verna (or Alverna). It was once owned by an Italian count named Orlando Cattani, but in 1213, the count donated the mountain to Francis and his monks as a place to go for silent prayer and contemplation. The count's note to Francis read,

"I have in Tuscany a faithful mount that is named Mount of La Vernia, which is really isolated and wild and perfect for those who want to do penance in a remote place or to those who want to live in solitude. If you would like it I will give it to you and your followers for my soul's safety."[89] Though the count had no way of knowing, the mountain he donated would become the site of a majestic miracle that would affect the lives of countless Catholics henceforth. For it was at La Verna that Francis received the stigmata.

While on retreat with Brother Leo at the hermitage in La Verna in September 1224, Francis prayed, asking God what his will was for him. Francis was undergoing significant physical pain—even by his standards. He felt that he was at a crossroads in his life and was faced with two possible choices: whether to live at the hermitage in prayer for the remainder of his life, or to continue evangelizing among the people.[90] Either way, Francis was entirely open to God's will, and prayed for a sign. To help find that sign, Francis turned to the Gospel and implored that God would communicate his will through a Gospel passage. He believed that whatever passage he came upon would contain the answer. So Francis opened the Gospel book. Thomas of Celano describes the scene: "And it happened, when he opened the book, that the first thing to meet his eye was the passion of our Lord Jesus Christ, and the passage saying that he would suffer a great ordeal. To avoid any suspicion that this was just coincidence, he opened the book a second and a third time, and found the same passage or a similar passage each time."[91] Though Francis understood that he was destined to undergo great suffering—and did not understand what form this suffering might take—he was joyful for obtaining clarity of God's will for him.

Shortly after that, Francis received a vision of a six-winged seraphic angel. This vision gave him a powerful consolation.[92] But it also made Francis sad. Because in the positioning of the man's arms and legs, it became clear to Francis that the angelic person was nailed to a cross. Francis was overcome with simultaneous happiness, sadness, and wonder, for he did not know what the vision meant. As he watched and wondered, he began to see that wounds appeared on his own body. Thomas of Celano describes, "His hands and feet seemed to be pierced by nails, the heads of the nails appearing on the inside of his hands and the upper side of his feet, and their points protruding on the other side. On the palms of his hands these marks were round, but on the outer side they were longer, and there were little pieces of flesh protruding from the surface which looked like the ends of nails, bent and hammered back."[93] But it was not just the hands and feet of Francis that bore wounds; it was his side as well. Thomas continues, "His right side was scarred as if it had been pierced by a spear."[94]

As in all things sent by God, Francis accepted the stigmata with happiness and gratitude. In fact, he was so overwhelmed with joy that he wrote a short piece to express his thoughts, known as *The Praises of God*.[95] Happily, we not only know the content of that composition; we have the actual original parchment written by "the stigmatized hand of Francis."[96] Today, the parchment is kept in Assisi, in the Basilica of St. Francis. Some parts of the writing on the parchment are illegible to the naked eye, and other parts are illegible even with the assistance of technology, but close examination of the original in comparison with existing copies renders this:

> You are the holy Lord God who does wonderful things.
> You are strong. You are great. You are the most high.
> You are the almighty king. You holy father,
> king of heaven and earth.

You are three and one, the Lord God of gods;
You are the good, all good, the highest good,
  Lord God living and true.
You are love, charity; you are wisdom.
You are humility, you are patience, you are beauty,
  you are meekness.
You are security, you are rest, you are gladness and joy,
  you are our hope.
You are justice, you are moderation,
  you are all our riches to sufficiency.
You are beauty, you are meekness.
You are our protector, you are our custodian
  and defender.
You are strength, you are refreshment.
You are our hope, you are our faith, you are our charity.
You are our sweetness, you are our eternal life:
Great and wonderful Lord, almighty God,
  merciful Savior.[97]

Francis gave the parchment to Brother Leo, and on the other side of that parchment is the firsthand testimony of Brother Leo, who writes, "Blessed Francis two years before his death kept a Lent in the place of Mount La Verna in honor of the Blessed Virgin Mary, the Mother of the Lord, and of the blessed Michael, the Archangel, from the feast of the Assumption of the holy Virgin Mary until the September feast of St. Michael. And the hand of the Lord was laid upon him; after the vision and speech of the Seraph and the impression of the stigmata of Christ in his body, he made and wrote with his own hand the *Praises* written on the other side of the sheet, giving thanks to the Lord for the benefits conferred on him."[98]

One might assume, especially considering his ebullient language in the *Praises*, that Francis would go out and proclaim his reception of the stigmata to the world; however, Francis was quiet about it. In fact, at first, he pondered the idea of being altogether silent regarding the stigmata. Not wishing to reveal his stigmata even to his religious brothers at first, he asked them an intentionally vague question about what to do in such a case. A brother named Illuminato answered Francis, "Brother, not only for thine own sake, but for the sake of others, thou knowest the divine mysteries are made known to thee. And therefore it seems to me that thou shouldst fear to conceal this which thou hast received for the benefit of many, lest thou shouldst be condemned for hiding the talent committed to thy care."[99]

Francis was convinced that Illuminato was correct in his assessment. Nevertheless, though Francis did allow some select others to see the stigmata, he was guarded. Bonaventure notes that Francis routinely covered his hands and wore sandals that covered the wounds on his feet. But as a practical matter, he had deep wounds in his hands and feet that bled, and needed bandages; such things cannot be easily hidden. Beyond that, he was in considerable pain from the wounds, and needed ongoing help from others.[100] Though it was covered, the wound in Francis's left side was perhaps the most difficult to hide since large amounts of blood seeped into his cassock. Following Francis's lead, his religious brothers at La Verna were also quiet about the stigmata.

Why all this secrecy? When searching for a motive for Francis, humility is always an excellent place to begin. How could Francis discuss his stigmata in a way that kept his humility intact? Beyond that, how could he properly and fully explain its significance? That would be no easy task. If someone received the stigmata today, at least there would be a precedent; obviously, this was not the case with Francis. Thus, as Fr. Solanus Benfatti, author of *The Five Wounds of Saint Francis,* points out, "At the very beginning, of course, it was as if Francis's stigmata were too new and shocking to be freely talked about."[101]

Notwithstanding the Franciscan secrecy, many people were not only aware of Francis's stigmata, but personally saw his wounds during Francis's life. Further, the list of eyewitnesses comprised some of the holiest and most trustworthy men in all of Christendom. Bonaventure notes that the list included many of his Franciscan brothers, who swore oaths that they had seen his stigmata. It also included multiple cardinals who not only saw his stigmata, but wrote about it. Beyond that, Pope Gregory IX was a personal friend of Francis, and canonized Francis less than two years after Francis's death—largely on the basis of the miraculous nature of his stigmata, and on the testimony of those who witnessed his stigmata.[102] Another eyewitness was the future Pope Alexander IV (who canonized St. Clare two years after her death). Bonaventure writes that the "supreme pontiff, Alexander, also, when preaching to the people, in the presence of many of the friars, of whom I was one, affirmed that, in the lifetime of the saint, he had seen the sacred stigmata with his own eyes."[103]

Beyond these dignitaries, many common people likely also saw Francis's stigmata. In the final months of his life, Francis continued missionary work in Italian towns and villages and returned to work for the lepers. It is important to note here that Francis had thousands of followers who regarded him as a living saint.[104]

Beyond those who witnessed the stigmata during Francis's life, more saw them at his death. Bonaventure notes that his wounds were seen by "more than fifty brethren together, and also by Clare, that virgin most devoted to God, with many of her sisters and an innumerable company of seculars, who, as will be seen hereafter, kissed them with great devotion and touched them with her hands, to ascertain the truth of the miracle, and the wound in the side also."[105] That scene was beautifully illustrated by Giotto's *Death of Saint Francis* in 1325.[106]

Francis lived for two more years after his miraculous reception of the stigmata in 1224. During Francis's final years, as Warren Carroll writes, "he reached the heights of spirituality perhaps never matched since the death of the beloved apostle."[107] Though Francis died on October 3, 1226, many miracles were attributed to Francis after his death—as we will examine in chapter 9.

CONCLUSION

We began this chapter with a series of questions, including this one: *who is God?* That is a pivotal question for everyone on earth; it is an immediate question for every Christian. Because if we seek to be Christ-like, we must seek to know Christ. For Francis, this thought defined him for the second half of his life. Truly, it would be hard to even know *how* to be more Christ-like, much less to *be* more Christ-like. Since Apostolic times, no one had done it better, so it is fitting that Francis was blessed with the stigmata. This raises an obvious question: *how can anyone match the holiness modeled for us by Francis?* In answer to that question, we should start with a rather obvious observation: there is only one Francis. Each person—stigmatist or otherwise—is unique; each one bears his or her own fingerprint of God. There is only one, unrepeatable Francis of Assisi. That uniqueness, however, does not negate similarity.

The goal of our Christian life is to imitate Christ, not to materially imitate the saints in every way. Still, as we continue our look at stigmatists, it will become clear that many possessed traits of holiness similar to those found in Francis. Among them, we can include: 1) an intense love of the Eucharist, 2) profound holiness, 3) a marked rejection of material things, 4) a deep desire to do the will of God, and 5) a transcendental personal devotion to the passion of Jesus. Among other circumstances and events, we might include the desire to hide the stigmata, at least initially, an intense suffering or near-death illness just prior to the reception of the stigmata, and a relatively early death.

Then there is the question: *Why were there no stigmatists for twelve centuries and so many thereafter?* God alone knows the reasons of his providential design, and why the stigmata would have begun at a particular point in time. Perhaps we can look for a partial answer in the insight of Brother Illuminato: "Father, know that it is not for yourself alone, but also for your neighbor, that the mysteries of heaven are unveiled to you." For twelve hundred years, Christianity was central to European life, but at the time of Francis's birth, men had begun to forget God; indeed, the church was falling into ruin. Francis helped to rebuild it—and restore the faith of those men lost in a wilderness of materialism. It would be reasonable to conclude that Francis was given the stigmata—at least in some measure—because men had forgotten God and how much God loves them. The stigmata are a visible reminder of Jesus' intense love for us. And men would need more reminders.

As we about to see, more stigmatists were on the way.

3

Three Hundred Stigmatists: Early Stigmatists in the Shadow of St. Francis

> Their existence is so well established historically that, as a general thing, they are no longer disputed by unbelievers, who now seek only to explain them naturally.
>
> —*The Catholic Encyclopedia*[108]

In the previous chapter, we investigated the stigmata of Francis—and referring to his five wounds as *stigmata* is certainly proper. Yet, it is also plain to see that St. Francis—who bore wounds on his hands and feet and side—did not have *all* the wounds of Christ. For example: Francis did not sweat blood, as Jesus did in the garden on Holy Thursday; patches of skin were not torn from his back, as Jesus suffered from the scourging; Francis did not bear wounds on his head, as Christ bore from the crown of thorns; he did not suffer from an agonizing shoulder wound, as Christ bore from carrying his cross; he did not suffer asphyxiation, as Jesus did on the cross. Pointing this out does not detract from

Francis in any way, but it does present us with a question: why these five wounds? Why did Francis not bear *all* the wounds of the Passion?

Let's try to examine the answer in the following way.

Stigmatists are graced to physically partake in the passion of Christ because their suffering illustrates God's love for the world—and the brutal death that he was willing to undergo to save men's souls. It is further contended that the wounds of stigmatists not only assisted in their salvation, but also led to the salvation of those around them who saw their wounds. For example, it seems reasonable to believe that by seeing five of the main wounds of the Passion exhibited by Francis of Assisi, men's hardened souls were softened, which helped lead to their salvation.

If that is true, however, why not replicate every wound Jesus endured? Aside from the practical impossibility, short of an ongoing miracle, of physically sustaining all the wounds of Jesus for any length of time and of maintaining any semblance of normal human interaction when so afflicted, the simple answer is that God in his Providence has willed these five wounds to be the enduring witness of Christ Crucified. When Jesus rose from the dead, the terrible wounds inflicted on his head and back and shoulders were no more—but the wounds in his hands and feet and side remained (Luke 24:40; John 20:20).

This being said, Jesus does reveal to the world the depth of his suffering in the Passion; that fact is evident from Scripture, Tradition, and the Magisterium—not to mention numerous private revelations and the otherwise-inexplicable Shroud of Turin. What one person cannot suffer without quickly succumbing to death, the stigmatists have collectively unveiled for us. One stigmatist bears wounds on his hands and feet and side; another on her head; still another sweats blood. Whether one wound of the Passion or many wounds, it is proper to call these miraculous wounds *stigmata*—the plural form of the Greek word *stigma*, meaning a mark on the body. The sacred and miraculous character of these marks on the bodies of stigmatists is our focus, not their exact number on any individual stigmatist.

Why take the time to make this distinction? Because some may discount stigmatists such as St. Lutgarde or St. Rita because these women did not bear the "full stigmata." As we have just illustrated, no one except Christ has borne—or can endure—the "full stigmata." But beyond that reality, this response badly misses a central point of the stigmata. Whether each stigmatist has endured one or several wounds of the Passion, the stigmatists in history have collectively illustrated something at least *approaching* the totality of our Lord's physical sufferings in his passion. As we will see, these stigmatists—though separated by countries and centuries—unite to illustrate the passionate mercy of Christ to the world. That is why, instead of focusing on one stigmatist, it is helpful to focus on many. And that is not difficult, since there were many. This chapter will focus on those the Catholic Church has formally recognized as saints, blessed, or venerable.

THE LENS OF CHRISTIAN SUFFERING

In the first chapter, we evoked the concept of compassion: *suffering together*. But to understand the stigmata and the motivations of the stigmatists, we must delve deeper now into the meaning of Christian suffering. Unfortunately, speaking about the meaning of Christian suffering is an unpopular topic in modern times. To the contemporary ear, hearing a nun pray for the grace of suffering can seem jarring and disturbing. Pain management has become a specialized medical field, and euthanasia is increasingly viewed as compassionate and assisted suicide as a human right.

In this environment, the idea of a person voluntarily suffering might seem bizarre, if not insane. To be sure, palliative care—treatment to lessen suffering—can undoubtedly constitute a noble and compassionate endeavor, especially when it recognizes the person's transcendental value and ontological dignity. After all, Christ healed the sick and suffering, and those who compassionately work to heal others are imitating Christ in their work. But our modern focus on relieving all pain at all costs has led to a painful and widespread epidemic: the addiction to painkillers. So, what is the Catholic notion of suffering? To understand the stigmata, it is essential to examine that question.

Some people might argue that even the *willingness to suffer* (or sacrifice, for that matter) constitutes mental illness. To address that, we can point out that many of us voluntarily and routinely undergo suffering and self-sacrifice—broadly defined—for those we love, but no one seriously posits that these actions constitute insanity. If a woman willingly suffers the pain of a syringe puncturing her arm to give blood to the Red Cross, does that indicate her insanity? If a woman enthusiastically becomes pregnant, knowing that she will eventually undergo the pains of childbirth, should we classify her as deranged? If a soldier freely suffers enemy bullet wounds and grenade shrapnel in the process of defending innocent people, is he crazy? If a man works on a construction site for eight hours on a hot day to support his family instead of going to the beach, is he a masochist? Clearly not.

But is there a way to distinguish between a reasonable act and a disordered act of suffering or sacrifice? Yes. These acts can be distinguished by what philosophers call their *end*. Aristotle and Aquinas explained that an "end" is the first thing intended, and last thing realized. Only a psychologically, spiritually, or emotionally disturbed person would seek pain because he enjoys pain as an *end*. It is perfectly natural, however, to recognize that one might need to undergo suffering or embrace sacrifice to achieve an end. Thus, the needle in the arm and childbirth pains are not ends—they are the *means* to an end. Though the Catholic may see the value in suffering, he does not believe suffering is the end. Quite the contrary: the last thing realized is not suffering, but rather, the vision of God in heaven. Lest we forget, there is no physical pain—or any other sort of pain—in heaven. All the humans and angels in heaven are privileged to see God as he truly is, and that vision produces complete and total happiness and inexhaustible joy of body, soul, and mind. That, not suffering, is the end—and every canonized stigmatist in heaven agreed with that sentiment quite precisely.

Of course, this prompts another question: conceding that suffering is not the *end*, why is suffering a *means* to salvation? As we mentioned earlier, all questions of theology seek to address one central interrogative: *who is God?* And with respect to human suffering, if God is perfectly good, why does he allow good men and women to suffer as the means to an end? More acutely, regarding the stigmata, why does God not only *allow* but *inflict* suffering on the best of men and women? To help answer that question, Pope St. John Paul II issued an apostolic letter titled *Salvifici Doloris* (SD), known in English by the title *On the Christian Meaning of Human Suffering*. Though the pontiff never directly mentioned the stigmata in this document, he makes several distinct points that prove valuable in our discussion.

First, John Paul notes that there is a "salvific meaning of suffering" (SD 1) and that we human persons can partake in the salvific suffering of Christ. Even most casual Gospel readers likely grasp that Jesus' suffering was somehow redemptive; it's hard to miss that the Resurrection followed

Good Friday. As John Paul writes, "Redemption was accomplished through the cross of Christ, that is, through his suffering" (SD 3). But does that mean anything to us in a practical, physical sense; that is, are we called to somehow partake in Jesus' suffering? St. Paul clarifies this question with a resounding affirmative; it reads, "I rejoice in my sufferings for your sake" (Col. 1:24).

Paul's letter informs us that our suffering has transcendental value when linked to the suffering of Christ. This constitutes a sea-change in the human understanding of suffering. In Old Testament times, people often understood suffering as punishment for sin. For example, the Book of Job relates that Job's associates frantically searched in vain for a terrible sin committed by Job to explain his suffering. Paul's letter informs us that some of the holiest and most innocent men and women also suffer; further, their suffering gains transcendental meaning and value when it is united with the suffering of Christ.

Second, our suffering helps us develop a more profound compassion for Jesus' sufferings, leading us to give ourselves more fully to him in love. Actual grace is a voluntary gift of God to help us achieve eternal happiness and a man's compassion toward Christ—especially in his passion—evidences a powerful grace. To illustrate the meaning of this sort of compassion, John Paul directs us toward the parable of the Good Samaritan. In the parable, a man has been beaten and robbed and left to suffer and die in a ditch. A priest sees the man but passes him by. Next, a Levite sees the man but goes out of his way to ignore him. But the grace of compassion moves the Samaritan, so he stops to check on the man. But the Samaritan goes even further. John Paul writes,

> The Good Samaritan of Christ's parable does not stop at sympathy and compassion alone. They become for him an incentive to actions aimed at bringing help to the injured man. In a word, then, a Good Samaritan is one who brings help in suffering, whatever its nature may be. . . . We can say that he gives himself, his very "I", opening this "I" to the other person. Here we touch upon one of the key-points of all Christian anthropology. Man cannot "fully find himself except through a sincere gift of himself" (SD 28).

Thus, perfect compassion is not only the willingness to suffer with Christ, but to give ourselves to him. John Paul writes, "Down through the centuries and generations it has been seen that *in suffering there is concealed* a particular *power that draws a person interiorly close to Christ,* a special grace. To this grace many saints, such as Francis of Assisi . . . owe their profound conversion" (SD 26). The same can be said of every saint and blessed who bore the stigmata.

Third, our suffering—when united with the cross of Jesus—can not only help us to achieve our own salvation, but also to assist in evangelizing and deepening the faith of others. Except in the hardest of hearts, seeing another person suffer evokes compassion, and this compassion can lead to a deep love and caring for the afflicted. Continuing his meditation on the Good Samaritan, John Paul expresses, "Following the parable of the Gospel, we could say that suffering, which is present under so many different forms in our human world, is also present in order *to unleash love in the human person*, that unselfish gift of one's 'I' on behalf of other people, especially those who suffer" (SD 29, emphasis in original).

Concerning the stigmata, this prompts the question: if we are moved to compassion in seeing the wounds of crucifixion on a stigmatist, who are we being compassionate *toward*? For many of those who see the wounds on the stigmatist, their compassion is directed not only to the stigmatist, but to Christ. In effect, the stigmatist is evangelizing with his or her suffering. Though some might view the stigmatists' wounds as grotesque, they are nonetheless *moving* and, in this way, stigmatists have brought others to Jesus in a response of love and compassion.

Fourth, our suffering can help expiate the sins of others, including both the souls in the Church Militant (the souls on earth) and the Church Suffering (the souls in Purgatory). Above, we read the first part of Paul's letter to the Colossians, but here is the entire verse: "Now I rejoice in my sufferings for your sake, and in my flesh I complete what is lacking in Christ's afflictions for the sake of his body, that is, the Church" (Col. 1:24). What does Scripture mean by "lacking?" Pope John Paul II explains:

> Does this mean that the redemption achieved by Christ is not complete? No. It only means that the redemption, accomplished through satisfactory love, *remains always open to all love* expressed in *human suffering*. In this dimension—the dimension of love—the redemption which has already been completely accomplished is, in a certain sense, constantly being accomplished (SD 24).

The fact that Christians can offer their suffering and penance for the sins of others is a practice well established in the Old Covenant, repeatedly reaffirmed in the New Covenant, Tradition, and the Magisterium. It is ingrained in the very sacramental life of the Church. As the *Catechism* explains,

"The Church, who through the bishop and his priests forgives sins in the name of Jesus Christ and determines the manner of satisfaction, also prays for the sinner and does penance with him" (1448).

J.K. Huysmans explains expiatory suffering well: "All through the ages there have been found saints willing to pay, by their sufferings, the ransom for the sins and faults of others."[109] Huysmans's book illustrates that, among the stigmatists who have suffered to expiate the sins of others, there is perhaps no greater example than that of St. Lydwine of Schiedam (1380-1433). Born in Holland during a time of civil brutality, openly scandalous lives of many prelates, widespread heresy, sacrilege against the sacraments, and the growing presence of Satanism, Lydwine took it upon herself to suffer for the poor souls of her entire nation.[110]

After a terrible ice-skating accident, Lydwine was confined to her bed for four decades, where she suffered a massive number of medical infirmities that included the Black Plague, an ulcer that destroyed all the skin on her right shoulder, gangrene, dropsy, huge ulcers, blindness in her right eye and near blindness in her left, numerous physical deformities that made her nearly unrecognizable, indescribably painful headaches, skin cancer, and kidney stones.[111] Over the span of thirty years, she ate almost nothing (except the Eucharist) and slept only a few hours *total* in that time.[112] Lydwine's overall condition was such that bandages were virtually holding her body together; in fact, her caregivers had to pay special attention while moving her, lest she literally fall apart.

As a young woman, Lydwine had felt abandoned by God, but a holy priest gave her advice that changed her life. He said, "Your vocation is clear; it consists in sacrificing yourself for others, in making reparation for faults you have not committed, in the practice of a sublime and truly divine charity."[113] For many years, not only Hollanders but people from all around Europe came to Lydwine's house to ask her to offer suffering for them—and that is precisely what she did. Lydwine had a particular devotion to the souls in Purgatory, many of whom were released due to her suffering on their behalf. (Of course, she also offered suffering for those painfully indifferent souls who never bothered to ask her.) Eventually, she received the stigmata, uniting her sufferings with those of Jesus.

Through this lens of Christian suffering, let's proceed.

THE FIVE MAIN WOUNDS

Many Catholics—not to mention non-Catholics—are unaware that anyone ever bore the mystical stigmata; moreover, even among those Catholics who have heard of the stigmata, it seems that only a tiny percentage know just how many of their fellow Catholics have suffered these wounds. One could perhaps name St. Francis and St. Padre Pio, but who else? Catholics may be shocked to hear the actual numbers. In 1912, *The Catholic Encyclopedia* noted that the Catholic Church had canonized or beatified sixty-two men and women who were reported to have the stigmata.[114]

We'll discuss later why that number was likely underestimated even at the time, but at this point, it is essential to understand that the number of beatified and canonized stigmatists is large enough to note certain similarities and differences among them. The majority of (beatified) blessed and (canonized) sainted stigmatists had wounds on their hands and feet as well as a wound in their sides. These are sometimes called the "five main wounds." But there were also stigmatists who exhibited only one wound. In the attempt to do justice to the stigmatists and the enormity of the wounds they suffered, we will focus on the individual wounds in the order that our Savior endured them. And as we progress, we need to highlight a central point: no two stigmatists experienced the same wounds in exactly the same way.

To understand the stigmata, it is also important to touch upon the reality of spiritual *ecstasy* because this is a prevalent feature in stigmatists. In modern times, the word *ecstasy* is often used in reference to an experience in which a person is hyperaware of his bodily pleasure, but that was not its original meaning; in fact, quite the opposite. The word comes from the Greek *ekstasis*, a derivative of *existánai*, meaning "displace, drive out of one's mind,"[115] in other words, *to displace the mind from one's physical surroundings.* Although the word can be used in a variety of ways, the *Catholic Encyclopedia* explains that *spiritual* ecstasies—those which concern us here—contain two main components.

The first is "interior and invisible, when the mind rivets its attention on a religious subject."[116] The second is "visible, when the activity of the senses is suspended, so that not only are external sensations incapable of influencing the soul, but considerable difficulty is experienced in awakening such sensation, and this whether the ecstatic himself desires to do so, or others attempt to quicken the organs into action."[117] We will discuss the subject of ecstasy in much more detail in the next chapter, but for the purposes of this chapter, we simply need to establish that the stigmatists often experienced these mystical ecstasies. For some of the stigmatists, the ecstasies lasted days at a time and were very common.

THE GETHSEMANE STIGMATA OF BLOOD

Catholic historians routinely hold that Francis was the first stigmatist. That statement is correct if we date the first stigmatist by the year of his birth: 1181. But the following year, a girl named Lutgarde was born in the town of Tongeren, in what is now the country of Belgium. And whereas Francis received his stigmata in 1224, Lutgarde had received her stigmata about fourteen years earlier. From that perspective and timeline, Lutgarde was granted the first known stigmata in history.

We have extensive details about Lutgarde, primarily due to her biography written by Thomas of Cantimpre, an Augustinian priest and one of the proficient writers of medieval Christendom. Thomas was her biographer and a personal friend who attested to the veracity of her stigmata. He recounts that Lutgarde was a Cistercian sister who, in her late twenties, would fall deeply in prayer and reflection about the passion of Jesus, earnestly desiring martyrdom like St. Agnes.

On one such occasion, she found herself so desirous of shedding her blood for Christ that a blood vessel near her heart ruptured—soaking her Cistercian tunic. A moment later, Christ appeared to her and said, "For the fervent desire for martyrdom you have shown in the shedding of your blood, you will receive in heaven the same reward for martyrdom that the most blessed Agnes received when her head was severed for my faith. For by your desire even to the shedding of blood you have equaled her martyrdom."[118]

There were two witnesses to the event; Thomas adds further evidence that the vein left a scar that remained throughout her life. Thomas attests that, after this occurrence and the appearance of Jesus, "whenever she was in a state of rapture and reflected on the passion of the Lord, her whole body appeared to her to be covered in blood."[119] Thomas recounts that a priest, who seemed skeptical and wished to get confirmation of these events, cut off some of her hair during one of these raptures and noticed that her "hair was soaked as if by dew with drops of blood."[120] It seems chronologically appropriate that the first stigmata reflected the sweating of blood (an event of Holy Thursday) followed fourteen years later by Francis's five stigmatic wounds (events of Good Friday). Rene Biot, author of *The Enigma of the Stigmata*, notes that this sort of stigmata manifestation was not unique to Lutgarde. For example, Bl. Catherine of Racconigi (1486–1574) exhibited a similar blood flow three centuries later.[121]

In the first chapter, we mentioned that sweating blood, while exceedingly rare, can sometimes be medically explained. Is it possible to distinguish between a natural occurrence and a miraculous one? There is plenty of room to argue where that separation should occur, but it seems that a fair way of distinguishing would be the timing of the sweating blood. Of the medically documented occurrences, it is difficult—if not impossible—to find a case of a person who sweats blood *on schedule*. For example, Venerable Maria Domenica Lazzeri (1815–1848), who had the main wounds of the stigmata as well as the crown of thorns, is reported to have sweat blood on Fridays.[122] In the few instances in which sweating blood naturally occurs, it is a largely unpredictable event brought on by hyper-panic. In some respects, it is medically similar to being scared to death. Who is scared to death on Friday nights, but only on Friday nights? Wouldn't the sort of person who falls into hyper-panic occasionally panic also on Monday mornings or Saturday afternoons? Unlike the characteristics one would expect in a person given to uncontrollable states of panic, the stigmatists are described as transcendentally peaceful and joyful most of the time. That is, they don't seem to have any of the conditions of nervous disorders—much less those disorders that are strong enough to produce a bloody sweat. Moreover, we might further note that it is difficult—if not impossible—

to find a medically explicable case of a person who sweats blood over the course of not days or weeks, but intermittently over *years*. And yet, some stigmatists did just that.[123]

THE STIGMATA OF SCOURGING

Among all the dozens of stigmatists who have been declared saint or blessed, the stigmata of *scourging* appears to be the rarest of the stigmatic injuries.

St. Colette of Corbie (1381–1447) is principally remembered as one of the most important influences of the Poor Clares, as she established many new convents and reformed existing ones. But she also had a tremendous devotion to the passion of Christ, and would commonly go into ecstasies focused on it. During one such ecstasy, Colette's "face swelled up as if it had been struck with many blows, seeming only to be of skin and bone. Her nose seemed all beaten out of shape. When she had ended her meditation, her face, as the sisters beheld her, resumed its former natural appearance. The swelling went away, and her nose took its old shape. It is plain St. Colette bore in her countenance the marks of the evil treatment our Lord received from the soldiers and his executioners."[124]

Anna Maria Gallo, who took the religious name of Sr. Mary Frances of the Five Wounds (1715-1791) when she became a Third Order Franciscan, was graced with the five main wounds of the stigmata. Before she received the stigmata, she mystically experienced the physical passion of Jesus on successive Fridays leading up to Good Friday. On the first Friday, she underwent the agony of Jesus in the garden and, on the following Friday, the suffering of scourging.

Bl. Anne Catherine Emmerich (1774–1824) suffered a wide array of stigmatic wounds, including the five main wounds. Three years before her death, she also suffered the wounds of scourging. Her biographer, Clemens Brentano, who was an eyewitness to her stigmata, writes, "On Friday, the 30th of March, at ten o'clock in the morning, she sank down senseless. Her face and bosom were bathed in blood, and her body appeared covered with bruises like what the blows of a whip would have inflicted."[125]

St. Gemma Galgani (1878–1903), who suffered the five main wounds, also experienced the wounds of scourging on at least four occasions during the Fridays of March 1901. These incidents were witnessed by others, and were progressively worse. The fourth Friday was the most dramatic. She had "wounds everywhere, that must have been nearly half an inch deep."[126] Nevertheless, some of her wounds vanished almost immediately afterward, and within three days, all her wounds had healed without a trace.

THE STIGMATA OF THORNS

Several among the saints and blessed recognized by the Church have exhibited mystical wounds of crowning with thorns.[127] These included Bl. Ida of Louvain (d. 1300), Bl. Osanna of Mantua (1449–1505), Bl. Anne Catherine Emmerich, St. Mary Francis of the Five Wounds, and others.[128] The biographer of Mary Francis, Fr. Daniel Farris, recounts, "The first time she shared in this mystery, great drops of blood streamed from her head, and the linen caps she wore were soaked with blood. Three of these caps were jealously preserved by Fr. Pessiri, to whom they had been left by Fr. Salvatore, her director, and to this day the blood-stains are distinctly visible upon them."[129]

In addition to these women, one saint's name in particular has become almost synonymous with the thorn stigmata: St. Rita of Cascia (1381–1457). After her husband and two sons died, Rita became an Augustinian sister in central Italy in 1413. Rita had a tremendous devotion to the passion of Jesus—praying to feel some element of what Jesus had suffered for her and the world. About thirty years after she entered the order, Rita was graced to hear a sermon by a Franciscan priest, who spoke about the sufferings of Jesus—heavily emphasizing the wounds of the crown of thorns. Moved to copious tears upon hearing the sermon, Rita prostrated herself before a crucifix and implored God:

> O my God and crucified Lord! O you who were innocent and without sin or crime! O you who have suffered so much for love of me! You have suffered arrest, buffeting, insults, a scourging, a crown of thorns, and finally a cruel death on the cross. Why do you wish that I, your unworthy servant, who was the cause of your sufferings and your pains, should have no share in your sufferings? Make me, O my sweet Jesus, a participant, if not of all of your passion, at least of a part of it. . . . I only ask you for one of the seventy-two thorns which pierced your head and caused you so much pain, so that I may feel a part of the pain you felt. O my loving Savior! Do not refuse me this favor. Do not deny me this grace. I will not leave here consoled, if you send me away without so desired a pledge of your love.[130]

Rita's prayer was answered. As she prayed before the crucifix, one of the thorns came out of the corpus of Jesus and was driven into her forehead.[131] Modern statutes and paintings of Rita are heavily sanitized, with her head wound being very slight, little more than an unsightly blemish.[132] But this was not the case. Her biographers note not only the immense suffering that this wound caused Rita, but two more characteristics of the wound: its horrifying ugliness and its overwhelming stench. The wound attracted worms who fed upon it, magnifying both her pain and the repulsiveness of the wound. All this made some other sisters nauseous to even be in Rita's presence.[133] Nevertheless, it seems that the sisters increased their love of Rita, as they were aware of the miraculous nature of her injury. But out of charity for her fellow sisters, Rita retreated to her tiny cell, where she spent her time in prayer.

By 1450, Rita had endured this thorn for nine years, during which the wound seemed to grow more painful, uglier, and even more fetid. The year 1450 was declared a jubilee year by Pope Nicholas V, and the sisters planned to make a pilgrimage to Rome for the graces. Of course, this presented a problem for Rita and her superior, who somewhat understandably did not want to show Rita and her wound to the people of Rome. So Rita prayed again for Jesus—if it be his will—to heal her wound so that she may make the trip. Again, Rita's prayer was answered: the wound miraculously vanished, and Rita made the pilgrimage with the other sisters. When she returned from Rome, the thorn and the pains returned the moment Rita passed through the doorway—but the pain was significantly worse. Rita endured the wound until her death seven years later.

It is curious that the year Rita died, Stephana Quinzani was born; Stephana also endured the thorn stigmata. But whereas Rita endured a single thorn, Bl. Stephana endured many, shedding much blood.[134] Every Friday, Stephana mystically underwent the successive physical pains of the Passion: sweating blood, then the scourging, the crowning, the nailing and hanging on the cross—a process that her confessor personally witnessed.[135]

St. Margaret Mary Alacoque (1647–1690) was a Visitation nun who is best known and loved among Catholics for her devotion to the Sacred Heart of Jesus; what is less than known is that she suffered from a stigmatic crown of thorns. When Margaret Mary was about thirty, Jesus appeared to her and placed a crown of thorns upon her head, saying, "My daughter, receive this crown as a sign of that which shall soon be given thee to render thee conformed to me."[136] From the moment that she willingly accepted that crown from the hands of Jesus, the pains from the stigmata were so intense that, as her biographer Bishop Emile Bougaud notes, "she could rest her head not even on her pillow."[137] Upon receiving her thorn stigmata, Margaret Mary responded, "I am more grateful to my sovereign master for this precious crown than if he had presented me the diamonds of the greatest monarchs of the world; and this so much the more, as no one can take it from me. Of necessity, it often affords me long hours of wakefulness in which to converse with the only object of my love; for, like my good master, who could not rest his adorable head on the bed of the cross, I am unable to rest mine on my pillow."[138]

Bl. Clara Isabella Fornari (1697–1744) experienced the five main wounds along with a unique version of the thorn stigmata. While Rita's thorn was lodged in her head, Clara's stigmata was manifested by thorns growing through her head and breaking loose—all this causing significant blood. As with some other stigmatists, Clara was physically assaulted by the devil in an effort to make her lose her faith; the devil even tempted her to commit suicide. Although demonic attacks against stigmatists are not unique, those against Clara were so strong that one of her biographers compared her combat with the devil to St. John Vianney's legendary encounters.[139]

Born near Nazareth, *St. Miriam Baouardy* (1846–1878) was a Greek Catholic whose parents died when she was only two years old, leaving her to be raised by her uncle. Like some other women stigmatists mentioned in this chapter, her uncle tried to set her up with an arranged marriage. But also, like many of the women stigmatists, she refused, explaining that she would devote herself to Christ in virginity. And though her uncle tried to force her to marry, she was adamant. When Miriam was twelve years old, one of her uncle's servants attempted to convert her to Islam. When she refused, saying, "I am a daughter of the Roman Catholic Apostolic Church," the servant slashed her throat with a scimitar and left her to bleed to death.[140] Mysteriously, as Miriam explained, "A nun dressed in blue picked me up and stitched my throat wound."[141] The woman also fed and cared for her for about a month in the grotto.

Beginning in Miriam's teen years and continuing after that, she experienced the five wounds of the stigmata, including the wounds of the crowning with thorns. As a special consolation, she also received confirmation of her choice of consecrated virginity in a mystical experience: "I then found myself in heaven with the Blessed Virgin, the angels and the saints. They treated me with great kindness. In their company were my parents. I saw the brilliant throne of the Most Holy Trinity and Jesus Christ in his humanity. There was no sun, no lamp, but everything was bright with light. Someone spoke to me. They said that I was a virgin, but that my book was not finished."[142] Indeed, her story was not finished, as Mariam lived to take her Carmelite vows at age 25. Her age at death was that of Christ: thirty-three years old. (Curiously, thirty-three was also the age of death of St. Clare of Montefalco, St. Catherine of Siena, and stigmatist Louise Lateau, whom we will read about in the next chapter. Venerable Maria Domenica Lazzeri died within days of achieving her thirty-third birthday.)

THE SHOULDER STIGMA OF CARRYING THE CROSS

Accompanied by two angels holding a cross, Jesus appeared to *Bl. Catherine of Racconigi* (1486–1574). Jesus lifted the cross from the angels and set it on her shoulder, saying: "This is the cross, my dear Spouse, which shall never forsake thee as long as thou livest. I give it thee now, for it becomes a Spouse who loves his dear Spouse faithfully to make her a present; it will seem very hard at first, but in the end, it will be very glorious."

Another Catherine blessed with the burden of the cross was *St. Catherine de Ricci* (1522–1590), a Third Order Dominican who lived among—and eventually headed—a community of contemplative Dominican women.[143] She was widely known and loved in the region she lived—so much so that people traveled long distances to see her. The events of her life regarding the stigmata are astonishing, even relative to her fellow stigmatists, and yet they are exceedingly well-documented by detailed first-person testimonies. Her biography was published within five years of her death, filled with eyewitness accounts, followed by another book written about thirty years after her death by a priest who had served Catherine's community during her life.

Catherine received the full stigmata at the age of twenty. Several months later, she received the thorn stigmata. Her companion sisters could sometimes observe the thorns in her head and sometimes only the blood from the wounds, but she suffered from them for nearly half a century.[144] Shortly after receiving the main five wounds and crown of thorns, Catherine was granted the shoulder stigma at around the age of twenty; she bore it for the rest of her life. Her biographer writes, "Yet one more symbol of her union with the Crucified was granted to Catherine, but one never visible except to the few who nursed her in her illnesses. This was a livid mark about three fingers wide, which went in a straight line from the top of her right shoulder, down her back to the waist; in which those privileged to behold it recognized, with deep reverence, the impression of the cross, as carried by our Savior from the Pretorium to Calvary."[145] Both the wound on her side and the marks on her shoulder were still visible in 1734—a year after her beatification—when her casket was opened to check for bodily incorruption.[146]

St. Veronica Giuliani (1660–1727) was a Capuchin Poor Clare nun who lived a life of extraordinary mysticism. Jesus and Mary both appeared to Veronica on multiple occasions. Several years after her final profession, she experienced a vision of Jesus carrying his cross. Jesus asked Veronica, "What do you desire?" Veronica answered, "This cross. And I long for this in order to be all yours and to love you!"[147] She saw Jesus' face covered with bloody sweat, and Veronica took that to mean that Jesus was "greatly offended by sinners." And Jesus asked her the same question again, to which Veronica answered, "I would like to prevent anyone from offending you." Jesus asked her for the third time, and Veronica replied, "My Lord, I desire nothing more than to do your will, to suffer for your love, and to be completely yours." In response, Jesus took the cross off his shoulder and put it on Veronica's shoulder.[148]

THE STIGMATA OF NAILS

As we have noted, it seems that the majority of the stigmatists have suffered from wounds on the hands and feet. However, simply describing them as "wounds" fails to provide the necessary description.

St. Francis of Assisi not only had lacerations on his hands and feet from which blood flowed, but appeared to have actual nails in those wounds that looked as though they had been hammered and bent back. Bonaventure writes,

> For there began immediately to appear in his hands and in his feet the appearance of nails, as he had now seen them in the vision of the Crucified. His hands and his feet appeared pierced through the midst with nails, the heads of the nails being seen in the insides of the hands and the upper part of the feet, and the points on the reverse side. The heads of the nails in the hands and feet were round and black, and the points somewhat long and bent, as if they had been turned back.[149]

Bonaventure's description provides a glimpse of not only Francis's condition, but also of Jesus' crucifixion. It makes sense that the Roman soldiers would have pounded nails into Jesus' hands and feet and then pounded in such a way as to bend the nails to prevent slippage or significant movement on the cross. Although other stigmatists shared the wounds on the hands and feet, this nail formation seems unique to Francis alone. As Fr. Herbert Thurston, author of *The Physical Phenomena of Mysticism,* writes, "In no one, so far as I am aware, of the fifty or sixty well-attested examples of visible stigmata which have been recorded during the past seven centuries, is anything to be met with which can be put in comparison with these rigid protruding nails."[150]

Bl. Gertrude of Delft (d. 1358) received the stigmata on Good Friday in 1340. The wounds regularly bled exactly seven times a day, which caused people to come to witness the wounds for themselves. Due to the fame, like many other stigmatists, Gertrude prayed for God to take away the visible signs. God answered her prayer by taking away the bleeding, yet the marks of the stigmata remained on her hands and feet.[151]

Bl. Osanna of Mantua (1449–1505) was granted the stigmata in her hands and feet when she was about thirty. The reception of those wounds was so intense that she cried out in agony and lost consciousness. Throughout the year, on Wednesdays and Fridays, and every day during Holy Week, her wounds appeared as though nails were about to burst through the skin.[152]

The increasing pain of the wounds on Fridays and during Holy Week was not uncommon for stigmatic wounds. *Bl. Luci of Narni* (1476–1544) had a similar experience. Like many other stigmatists, Luci received the wounds on her hands, feet, and side as she was in deep contemplation of Jesus' passion. She tried to hide her wounds, but to no avail due to copious bleeding. Ecclesiastical authorities launched numerous investigations, including one conducted by Pope Alexander VI's personal physician, who confirmed their miraculous nature.[153] Because the stigmata were causing great adulation and fame, Lucy prayed that her wounds would disappear from the sight of others. God granted Lucy's request with a twist: the wounds on her hands and feet disappeared, but the wound in her side—out of the sight of others—remained.[154] Though many made pilgrimages to see Lucy, some penultimately hated her—and ultimately, hated Christ. An attempt was even made on her life.[155]

After Lucy's stigmata vanished from sight, a story was fabricated that her stigmata were self-inflicted, and she was broadly shunned in her convent for the last four decades of her life. Historian Edmund Gardner describes that "the nuns kept her a close prisoner in the convent, humiliating her in every possible way, treating her as an impostor and criminal."[156] However, she suffered the terrible injustice with august dignity and never complained.[157] Lucy's biographer, Georgiana Fullerton, writes, "During the whole remaining period of her life, a space of eight-and-thirty years, she bore her heavy cross without a murmur. . . . Her life was a long prayer for her persecutors."[158] But after her death, Lucy's body proclaimed her innocence and truthfulness to a guilty and dishonest world. When preparing her for burial, the wound in her side was discovered—a wound that was "dripping with fresh wet blood."[159] In 1710—over a century and a half after her death—her casket was opened, revealing that she was incorrupt, complete with marks of the stigmata visible to all.[160]

St. Marguerite Bays (1815–1879) was a Swiss seamstress who received the stigmata after a miraculous stomach cancer cure. (The granting of the stigmata after overcoming a life-threatening illness is emblematic of many stigmatists; perhaps illness serves as a trial allowed by God to test the person before the stigmata is granted.) Her cure has another fascinating detail. Bays had a deep devotion to Mary, and—mysteriously—she was cured of cancer on the exact day that Pope Pius IX formally pronounced the dogma of the Immaculate Conception: December 8, 1854. She had the stigmata of the main wounds, which appeared and disappeared, with her stigmatic pain coming particularly on Good Fridays. In what should come as no surprise, Marguerite died at 3 p.m. on a Friday—the octave of the solemnity of the Sacred Heart of Jesus.[161]

Whereas Francis had nails that appeared to have grown into the wounds in his hands and feet, other stigmatists simply had a thin membrane of skin or holes where the nails would have gone. Catherine de Ricci's fellow sisters observed that they could see through the holes in her feet.[162] The same is true for *St. Mary Frances of the Five Wounds.* In sworn testimony for the latter's beatification investigation, her confessor Don Paschal Nitti stated,

> I have seen them, I have touched them, and to say the truth I, as the apostle St. Thomas did, have put in my finger into the wounds of her hands and I have seen that the hole extended right through, for in inserting my first finger into the wound it met the thumb which I held underneath on the other side of the hand. . . . And this experiment I have made in many Lents, and on many Fridays in March, because it was on such days that the said wounds were most fully developed.[163]

Medical testimony exists that confirmed a similar condition in the case of *St. Padre Pio* (1887–1968). One of the physicians who inspected him stated, "So great is my certainty, that if authorities were to question me on this point, I could reply under oath that I could see, in transparency, some kind of object through the holes in his hands."[164]

THE WOUND OF THE LANCE: THE HEART STIGMA

There have been stigmatists who have endured what has been termed a "heart stigma," that is, a wound on the heart that seems to be caused by a lance. This wound is unique among the stigmata because it is the one wound that Jesus did not physically suffer; we have it on the authority of Scripture that Jesus died *before* the lance was driven into his precious body. Nevertheless, the lance caused a wound, one that remained in his glorified body at the Resurrection. We know this because, one week after the Resurrection, Jesus invited Thomas the apostle to put his hand into his side. The image on the Shroud of Turin and the science of cardiology (as we discussed in chapter 1) illustrates that the wound was on Jesus' right side.

As Pierre Barbet explains, "The shroud bears clear marks of this wound on the left side, and as the images are reversed, this means that it was on the right."[165] Barbet further explains that the Roman soldier drove his lance through Jesus' side, all the way to the "right auricle . . . perforating the pericardium" of his Sacred Heart, where blood and water gushed forth.[166] We often refer to this as a "side wound," but that terminology is incomplete. For example, if a patient today were stabbed so deeply through the ribs that his heart was punctured, no physician would refer to this merely as a "side wound" for the simple fact that the wound in the side would be a comparatively minor injury to a heart wound. The critical point is that the soldier's lance drove all the way to Jesus' Sacred Heart. Thus, it would be preferable to refer to this not as a *side wound* but as a *heart wound.*[167] By extension, those who mystically bear this heart wound bear the Lord's *heart stigma.*

The earliest occurrence of a heart stigma comes from St. Gertrude the Great (1256-1302). Gertrude was born in Germany in 1256—thirty years after the death of Francis of Assisi. We can deduce from her writings that she was orphaned.[168] What we know about Gertrude's early childhood is that she was born on the Feast of the Epiphany and that she was taken in and raised by the sisters of the Benedictine Abbey at the age of five, where she later joined as a professed member once she had attained the required age.

Over the years, she proved brilliant to her teachers—excelling in her courses in philosophy and becoming so fluent in Latin that she could conduct conversations in the ancient language. Her mental gifts were so clear that she rapidly moved from student to teacher within her order. By her twenties, Gertrude had become renowned for her intelligence and wisdom. As biographer Gilbert Dolan notes, "Her learning became famous far beyond the walls of her own monastery, and many came even from distant parts to consult her on difficult subjects."[169] But her holiness, affection, and devotion to God towered above her academic achievements. The sisters noticed that Gertrude's prayers had extraordinary efficacy.[170]

To read the biographical and autobiographical accounts of Gertrude is to marvel at the indescribable love that Jesus had for her, and that she—challenging the limitations of fallen human nature—had for Jesus. One of the most apparent indications of that love was that Jesus began appearing to Gertrude when she was twenty-five years old. A few months after the first apparition, she felt a wound upon her heart. She writes, "I felt, O my God, how thou didst imprint on my heart thy adorable wounds, even as they are on thy sacred body."

The tremendous pain from this endured until her death. Seven years after this first stigmata event, a second one occurred as she prayed in church after receiving Holy Communion. She writes, "After I had received the sacrament of life, I saw a ray of light, like an arrow, dart forth from the sacred wound in thy right side, on the crucifix. . . . It advanced toward me and pierced my heart. Then thou didst say to me: 'May the full tide of thy affection rise to me, so that all thy pleasure, thy hope, thy joy, thy grief, thy fear and every other feeling may be sustained by my love!'"

In 1268, while Gertrude was mastering Latin as a twelve-year-old in Germany, a girl named *Clare* was born in Montefalco, Italy—a little town about ten miles south of Assisi. When a child is particularly gifted with a genius in music or art, we sometimes refer to that child as a "prodigy." In that respect, we might call little Clare a Christian prodigy. Even at the age of four, Clare displayed a deep devotion to the passion of Jesus and would spend as much as four hours at a time in prayer and contemplation.[171] Clare visited Montefalco's hermitages and learned about God. When Clare was still very young, her older sister Johanna founded a little hermitage, where she planned to withdraw from the world and live a life of prayer and austerity with other religious sisters. Tiny Clare was convinced that she should join her sister.

Understandably, Johanna refused to admit her sister—sincerity notwithstanding. But Clare was resolved and prayed that she could gain admission. Johanna eventually changed her mind and admitted Clare with the approval of the local bishop of Spoleto. Thus, Clare grew up in the hermitage.

By 1290, the little hermitage had grown in number considerably, and it was clear to the sisters that they should join a formally approved religious order. Seeking the counsel of their bishop, the sisters joined the Augustinian order, and Johanna was selected to be the first abbess.[172] Sadly, Johanna died the very next year, leaving Clare in profound grief and sadness. As Jesus wept over Lazarus, Clare wept over Johanna. The heartache over the loss of her sister led Clare to cry uncontrollably for three days.

On the third day, as Clare was in prayer, she heard a voice calling her name. She recognized the voice as Johanna's. Clare was amazed, and responded to the voice, "My dear sister, are you then not dead?" The voice answered, "Yes, I am dead; but my death has been simply a transition to paradise, where I shall enjoy my God for ever."[173] St. Clare's chief biographer explains that "Clare heard the voice, but saw only a large flame, which finally approached and settled on her head. She then felt a holy calm suddenly take possession of her heart, and her sorrow was changed into joy and feelings of gratitude toward God."[174] Although Clare was only in her early twenties, and her humility led her to resist the job, the sisters unanimously elected her as the new abbess.[175]

As the abbess, Clare's contemplations and prayers—indeed her entire being—remained focused on the same subject as since childhood: the passion of Jesus. One of her biographers notes that Jesus' passion "was in her thoughts night and day; always on her lips in her instructions to the nuns. She had made it a special prayer that she might be granted to see in spirit all that he had suffered on Calvary and the road that led to Calvary."[176] But the answer to her prayer went beyond suffering in spirit; she would suffer physically. Ten years after her election, at the age of thirty-three, Clare was in an ecstasy in which she saw a vision of Jesus, who was carrying a large cross. And Jesus said to her, "I have been looking for a spot where I can plant my cross. Thy heart is a fitting place; suffer it to take root there."[177] From that moment until her death seven years later, Clare endured the heart stigma.

In her final days, Clare spoke about the wound with the sisters. One of the sisters asked Clare if she was afraid of dying. Clare answered, "Of whom should I be afraid, since I have my crucified Jesus within my heart?"[178] And then, in the final moments in her earthly life, after the viaticum and anointing of the sick, Clare made what might have been considered a rather bold statement to her sisters: "You will find the cross of Jesus graven on my heart."[179] This prediction would encourage the faith of the sisters and many faithful Christians for all the following centuries. She died shortly after that in the presence of her religious sisters. St. Clare of Montefalco was forty years old.

Less than forty years after Clare's death, *St. Catherine of Siena* (1347–1380) was born. Catherine was one of the most magnificent lights in the history of Christendom, a fact recognized by her official declaration as a Doctor of the Church. Catherine experienced all five main wounds but was particularly pained by the heart wound. We have a firsthand account of how she received the stigmata since her confessor, Bl. Raymond of Capua, wrote a biography of Catherine at the pope's request.[180]

During a Sunday Mass in mid-Lent, Catherine received Holy Communion and went into ecstasy. After some time, Catherine fell to the ground as if struck dead. A few moments later, Catherine described to Fr. Raymond what had occurred, telling him that "by the mercy of the Lord Jesus, I now bear in my body his stigmata."[181] She told Fr. Raymond that she had seen a vision of Jesus on the cross, leaning toward her with shining lights directed toward her hands, feet, and heart. Catherine knew that she was receiving the stigmata and spoke to Jesus, begging him that the stigmata be not visible on her body. When Catherine came out of the ecstasy, she was in terrible pain—nevertheless, no wounds appeared on her body. Jesus had answered her request—that if she were to experience the stigmata, it would be invisible. I feel such pain at those five points, especially in my heart, that if the Lord does not perform another miracle I do not see how I can possibly go on, and within a few days I shall be dead."[182] In the week following this event, her friends were afraid that she would die; nevertheless, Catherine did survive.

St. Teresa of Ávila, one of the greatest minds in the history of Christendom and the founder of the Discalced Carmelites, recounted a similar event in her autobiography. Around the year 1560, Teresa had a vision of a beautiful angel: "In his hands I saw a great golden spear, and at the iron tip there appeared to be a point of fire. This he plunged into my heart several times so that it penetrated to my entrails. When he pulled it out, I felt that he took them with it, and left me utterly consumed by the great love of God. The pain was so severe that it made me utter several moans."[183] And yet, at the same time, she tells us that "the sweetness caused by this intense pain is so extreme that one cannot possibly wish it to cease, nor is one's soul then content with anything but God. This is not a physical, but a spiritual pain, though the body has some share in it—even a considerable share."[184]

Like Catherine's, Teresa's heart stigma could not be seen. She presumed that some would accuse her of fraud. This troubled her, not for the sake of her glory, but because their doubt would deprive them of their benefit resulting from belief. Thus, in contrast to Catherine of Siena, Teresa prayed that others might see the truth in her account. Teresa continued, "So gentle is this wooing which takes place between God and the soul that if anyone thinks I am lying, I pray God, in his goodness, to grant him some experience of it."[185] Her prayer was answered. A postmortem examination clearly showed a slit in her heart that appeared to be caused by a sharp instrument; further, her heart survives in a reliquary, and that cut in her heart can still be seen.[186]

St. Charles of Sezze (1613–1670) was a Franciscan friar who recounted the reception of the stigmata in his autobiography. He was meticulous in describing it as a case of heart stigma—as opposed only to a wound in his side. The event occurred at the moment of consecration during Mass when Charles was about thirty-five years old. He writes, "When the priest lifted the consecrated host, with the eyes of my soul I saw streaming from it a ray of light that came and struck my heart. . . . I had been pierced by the hand of our Lord with the dart of his love. . . . But though the pain was great it was tempered by an excessive sweetness that penetrated the very depth of my soul."[187] His wound lasted three years.[188]

The Christian who tries very hard to *believe* and the skeptic who tries very hard to *disbelieve* might be concerned by a lack of evidence for these claims, considering that *anyone* could perhaps claim that he suffered from a heart stigma or invisible stigmata for the simple reason that no one would ever see it. But people *did* see these wounds. We've discussed some of these incidents and their witnesses, but one of the most remarkable concerns *St. Veronica Giuliani.*

Many years before she died in 1727, Veronica Giuliani explained that she had tiny images of the instruments of Jesus' passion physically *imprinted* upon her heart. That was quite a claim for two main reasons: first, that the imprints should exist in the first place; second, that Veronica should somehow know they were there. As we have seen, to be a stigmatist is to endure mountains of doubts and allegations of fraud or insanity. Still, even a passionate atheist should be able to admit that this sort of heart stigma is impossible to fake. A woman could drive nails through her own hands and feet, but how would she give herself heart surgery? No one in history successfully performed a heart surgery on another person until 1893—over a century and a half after Veronica's death.[189] What they did have in 1727 was autopsies. When a surgeon performed an autopsy on Veronica in the presence of numerous people, they attested to seeing the same image on her right ventricle that Veronica had drawn.[190]

A FINAL WORD ON SUFFERING AND STIGMATA

One last note on suffering, and it is a vital one. Some of the Catholic faithful in history—including some of the stigmatists—also practiced severe austerities that might shock us today. For an early period of her life, Veronica Giuliani—for instance—inflicted terrible wounds upon her body. As her biographer Bret Thoman writes, "Veronica took on extra penances that were more severe than ordinary fasting and the disciplines established by the Capuchin constitutions. Her description of these events is not easy to read. On the contrary, it is shockingly violent and sometimes bloody."[191] It is one thing to forgo a mattress and sleep on a bare floor, or to suffer from the flu and offer those sufferings for the souls in purgatory, but quite another to whip oneself with cords to the point of injury.

We must remember that the Catholic Church canonizes sinners—*repentant* sinners, to be sure, but sinners nevertheless—and even the saints were sometimes excessive to the point of objective fault. We must also bear in mind that, for centuries, corporal penances were an accepted and sometimes prescribed method of mortification even in many religious institutes. In medieval times, the dividing line between virtuous self-abasement and vicious self-harm seemed difficult to discern. Thoman explains,

> Regarding the intensity of her penances, it should be noted that Veronica was formed in a cultural and religious milieu that is three centuries removed from our own. Her formation and spirituality were affected by her family, her confessors and spiritual directors, the history of her era, and the books she read. It was the Baroque era, in which piety was focused on the cross, and popular religiosity expressed itself in corporal penances informed by fear of God and his punishments. It is not unreasonable to suggest that Jansenism and Quietism were at work in the monasteries of that era (and in the life of Veronica Giuliani)—both movements condemned by popes.[192]

The heresy of Jansenism sought to motivate by fear of an angry God, and that view of God sometimes translated into drastic penances.

Thoman offers another vital observation: after she received the stigmata, Veronica *ceased these terrible mortifications.* He writes, "After receiving the stigmata, Veronica underwent a significant change in her penances. She stopped inflicting them on herself. From that date, her diary no longer contains descriptions of external or voluntary sufferings. She realized that intense penances had little to do with daily life."[193] Insofar as we seek to understand the stigmata and the stigmatists, and insofar as we strive to imitate them, we must be aware of this.

Crosses surround us Christians without our needing to hunt for them. Padre Pio, a stigmatist we will discuss in the next chapter, clarified this point. He was once asked what penances he imposed upon himself above those instructed by his Capuchin order. He answered, "None: I take the ones the Lord sends."[194] When we carry our crosses, we must be motivated by love—and an unshakable confidence that God loves us. That is the message of the stigmata.

CONCLUSION

After looking at many of the stigmatists from the time of Francis to the mid-1850s, we can see some common denominators. First, all the stigmatists were mystics. Specifically, each seems to have experienced mystical ecstasy; many had visions and even discussions with Jesus and the saints; many experienced mystical marriage; and—of course—receiving the stigmata is itself a mystical experience.

Second, all the stigmatists had an intense devotion—coupled with empathy, in its most real sense—to the passion of Jesus.

Third, all the stigmatists excelled in holiness and virtue. The substance of that claim is borne out in the fact that the stigmatic saints were not beatified or canonized *because of* their mystical wounds (although this may have influenced some of these declarations). Even the canonization decree for Francis is silent about his stigmata. Simply, the great holiness of these men and women was evident apart from their wounds. Though the stigmata brought these men and women closer to Jesus, the stigmata were given to those *already* exceptionally close to Jesus.

Fourth, all the stigmatists had a powerful love of the Eucharist. This point is crucial to understanding both the stigmata and the stigmatist, and will be the subject of chapter 5.

And fifth, many had an illness that preceded the reception of the stigmata. Although time and space do not allow us to go into detail on this point, it should nevertheless be recognized that the stigmatists shared a feature that is often overlooked. Just days or weeks before many of them were marked with the stigmata, they underwent a life-threatening illness, only to suddenly recover. Perhaps God desired them to receive the sacrament of anointing of the sick just prior to the stigmata, or perhaps God was testing their ability to suffer with love and peace. Whatever the reason, it's essential to recognize this fact, which will be an area of discussion in the next chapter.

Although it is not a common denominator, a cumulative gaze at the stigmatists reveals a striking fact: roughly 90 percent of the saints and blessed reported to have borne the stigmata are women. We can speculate why that is the case, but there is no sure answer. It is tempting to wonder if the answer lies in the fact that women—most notably our Blessed Mother—were at the foot of the cross, while only one of the apostles was present. We may also wonder if the answer can be found in the longings of the Blessed Virgin Mary herself, who desperately wanted to suffer with her Son. In suffering the wounds of the Passion, the stigmatists were not only imitating Christ in the pain of the Passion, but also Mary, who desired to suffer with him.

Alongside these similarities among the stigmatists, we must also recognize the differences. We have already highlighted that no two stigmata were precisely the same: the wounds varied, the visibility varied, the appearance of the wounds after death varied, the pain varied, and so forth. But there are other differences. Some received the stigmata at a very young age; some received it at an old age. Bl. Stephania Quinzani received the stigmata at age fourteen, whereas Ven. Ursula Benincasa was sixty-six.[195] Some bore the stigmata for a comparatively short time; others for decades. For example, Francis of Assisi bore the stigmata for only two years; Catherine de Ricci for nearly fifty.[196] Some stigmatists were cloistered; some were not. A wide variety of religious orders are represented: Franciscans, Poor Clares, Jesuits, Visitandines, Dominicans, or Cistercians. Though most stigmatists joined religious orders at a young age, stigmata were not exclusive to virgins and the unmarried. Bl. Luci of Narni was married. St. Rita was married and had two sons. Bl. Marie of the Incarnation (1566–1618) was married with six children and would go into ecstasies while saying the rosary with her family.[197] Bl. Elizabeth Canori Mora (1774–1825) was married and bore four daughters.

Similarities and differences aside, just how many men and women are reported to have been given the mystical stigmata? Earlier in this chapter, we referred to the *Catholic Encyclopedia,* which listed the number of blessed and canonized men and women as sixty-two. That figure is low for several reasons.

One reason is that more stigmatists have been beatified and canonized since the *Catholic Encyclopedia* was published in 1911. Among the stigmatists, we can cite the following examples:

- Pope Benedict XV beatified Bl. Anna Maria Taigi in 1920.
- Pope Pius XII canonized St. Gemma Galgani in 1940.
- Pope John XXIII canonized St. Charles of Sezze in 1959.
- Pope St. John Paul II beatified Bl. Agnes of Jesus in 1994, Bl. Anna Rose Gattorno (1831–1900) in 2000, and canonized St. Padre Pio in 2002.
- Pope Benedict XVI canonized St. Camilla Battista Varani (1458–1524) in 2010.
- Pope Francis canonized St. Angela of Foligno (1248–1309) in 2013, St. Miriam Baouardy (1846–1878) in 2015, and St. Marguerite Bays (1815–1879) in 2019.

Thus, even if the *Catholic Encyclopedia*'s number was correct in 1911, it is outdated now.

A second reason is that, as the dates above illustrate, some canonizations do not occur until many centuries after the person's death. Over seven hundred years passed from the time of St. Angela's death to her canonization. Of course, this waiting period is not just a unique predicament for the stigmatic saints; it is much more universal. Many canonizations take centuries: for instance, St. Joan of Arc died in 1431 but was not canonized until 1920. St. Juan Diego died in 1548 but was not canonized until 2002. Couple this waiting period with the fact that most saints are not well known until their canonizations, and we can arrive at a probable conclusion: more men and women stigmatists will likely be declared blessed or canonized. It is highly likely that there have been dozens of stigmatists who have already lived and died who will be declared saints one day.

Finally, and this point needs to be emphasized, the Catholic Church may have already canonized stigmatists without our being aware of their stigmata. Many of the blessed and canonized stigmatists—at least initially—did not want others to know that they bore the mystical stigmata. We saw that in the case of St. Francis, and his desire for secrecy was commonly shared with his fellow stigmatists, as we saw in the case of St. Catherine of Siena, who prayed for her stigmata to become invisible. The stigmata are hard to hide, but not impossible—especially within the cloistered walls of a monastery or convent. Did an unknown Cistercian woman in the fourteenth century bear the heart stigma? Did an Egyptian desert hermit bear the mystical crown of thorns in solitude? We know about the men and women who could not keep their stigmata a secret, but were others successful in their concealment?

When we ponder this question, we might wonder about specific saints. For instance, it is curious that St. Thomas Aquinas was such a prolific writer but stopped writing after he had the mystical experience of Jesus speaking to him from a crucifix. That mystical experience is precisely the event that usually precedes the reception of the stigmata. Also taking into account Thomas Aquinas's love of the Eucharist and devotion to the Passion, along with the prevalence of Dominicans who have received the stigmata, we might ask: why *not* Aquinas? Perhaps he had invisible stigmata like St. Catherine of Siena or St. John of God (1495–1550).[198] We can only speculate about Aquinas, but the fact remains that it is certainly possible that some saint(s) had the stigmata that we are simply unaware of.

Beyond those who have been beatified or canonized, the more expansive question about the total number of stigmatists in history is undoubtedly a cause for wonder. In the late nineteenth century, there was a French physician named Antoine Imbert-Gourbeyre who deeply wondered. He met a woman who exhibited the stigmata, and was so fascinated by her and her wounds that he took it upon himself to exhaustively research the total number of those who had credible accounts of having the stigmata from the time of St. Francis to his day. He documented the total number at an astonishing three hundred and twenty-one.

Until this point in the book, we have almost exclusively referenced those blessed or canonized. But as we move forward closer to our day, it is essential to examine the lives of modern stigmatists—some of whom have not been (at least, not *yet* been) canonized, but whose stories are highly credible. One of the most important reasons to read these accounts is that modern stigmatists shine a light on critical medical aspects of the stigmata. In the following chapter, we will see that medical science helps confirm the miraculous nature of the mystical stigmata. From a medical perspective, the year 1850 provides a reasonable line of demarcation between the early and modern stigmatists, for it was in that year that the woman whose stigmata so enthralled Dr. Gourbeyre was born.

Her name was Louise Lateau.

4

SCIENCE, SKEPTICISM, SCRUTINY, AND FAITH: THE AGE OF MODERN STIGMATISTS

I have witnessed highly extraordinary things, commonly referred to as miracles. I will recount them.

Free-thinkers delight in denying this order of facts, contesting their existence and even their possibility. However, this denial is always asserted without good faith, without science, and also without success. The denial of the supernatural is a very old illness, uniquely aggravated in our time. The more one obstinately denies miracles, the more they occur on a vast scale: never in France have we witnessed more supernatural events occur than in the past fifty years.

—Antoine Imbert-Gourbeyre[199]

When analyzing the stigmata and their history, the year 1850 provides a natural line of demarcation between the stigmatists of old and modern stigmatists. This is true for five main reasons.

First, a Belgian girl named Louise Lateau was born in 1850. Lateau's wounds of the stigmata captured the attention of the medical world not only in her native Belgium but around the globe. For instance, numerous accounts of her case were even reported in *The New York Times*. To that point in time, no stigmatist in history had ever received as much attention. Because her stigmata lasted for fifteen years, and because several hundred doctors examined her and printed their findings in numerous nations, Lateau's case amounted to a new epoch in the history of the stigmata.

Second, one of the physicians who observed her case, Antoine Imbert-Gourbeyre, became a powerful advocate of Lateau, which led him to do extensive research and write about the history of the stigmata. By providing a chronology of the incidents of the stigmata along with biographies of three hundred and twenty-one stigmatists, Imbert-Gourbeyre became one of the greatest champions of the stigmata in history. He documented that the phenomenon was not exclusive to just two or three persons but to hundreds of women and dozens of men. Though he infuriated some of his medical colleagues in doing so, he advanced the position that the stigmata themselves are a supernatural occurrence that can only be appropriately analyzed within the field of mystical theology.

Third, due to the growing prevalence of Marxism among what Tom Wolfe later termed the "radical chic" intellectual class and facing Imbert-Gourbeyre's countering influence, the nineteenth-century men of science and medicine became open enemies of the stigmatists. Only six years before Lateau's birth, Karl Marx declared, "Religion is the sigh of the oppressed creature, the heart of a heartless world, and the soul of soulless conditions. It is the *opium* of the people."[200] Thus, those who possessed the stigmata and those who believed them were deemed enemies. This marked a new stage in the history of the stigmata. In the previous chapter, we discussed how many stigmatists had their share of doubters. Some were treated terribly even by—*especially* by—members of their own religious orders. Most were not oppressed outside their communities or orders as they remained within those dwellings. (Sadly, there were striking exceptions, such as St. Lydwine, who was nearly murdered in her own house.) But during and after the Age of Enlightenment, stigmatists—along with the very concept of the stigmata—were viciously bullied and attacked by broader society.

The country of France provides an excellent example. In the late eighteenth century and following, Catholic priests and laity were executed for the crime of being Catholic because practicing the faith upset the apple carts of atheism and socialism. While some apostatizing priests scandalously swore allegiance to the guillotining French revolutionaries, faithful French priests bore the brunt of their malice, and hundreds were put to death. Thus, in so-called "enlightened" societies, it is little wonder that Catholic stigmatists suffered ridicule, bullying, and government harassment. The widespread influence of Marxism in Europe simply picked up the baton from the French revolutionaries years prior, and the intellectuals put the stigmatists in their crosshairs.

Fourth, there were considerable advances in medicine during this time. In the mid-1800s, significant discoveries such as Louis Pasteur's germ theory and the use of antiseptics had immediate application to possible medical explanations of the stigmata. But if the free-thinking doctors thought that medical discoveries would serve to refute the mystical stigmata, they were wrong. In many ways, modern medicine only served to confirm their supernaturality. (The advances in stigmatically relevant medical discoveries will be detailed in chapter 7.)

Fifth, the invention of the camera made it possible to reproduce images of the stigmatists' wounds. In a world of smartphones, it's easy to lose sight of the fact that cameras were not commercially available until 1839, and even those were extremely rudimentary.[201] However, as the process of photography improved over the next few years, photographs had a tremendous influence on the public. For the first time, scenes from a war—America's Civil War—were captured on film, forever influencing not only America's impression of war but of policy toward war. The pictures of the stigmatists made it broadly known that people suffered—or, at least, claimed to suffer—from the wounds of the stigmata. Obviously, we do not have photographs of St. Francis and his stigmata, but we do have a series of photos of Louise Lateau. Though some might argue that a picture is inconclusive, it is nevertheless indisputable that the 1877 photos of Louise Lateau brought the discussion of the stigmata to the global forefront.[202]

We must consider these factors as we move forward with our discussion of the stigmata. We will begin our discussion with Louise Lateau and Dr. Antoine Imbert-Gourbeyre. Their biographies, their treatment by the medical community, and their encounters with free-thinkers provide fascinating insights into the modern stigmatists, the way stigmatists are often treated, and why Catholics must defend the wounds of Jesus and those who bear them. Beyond that, we will discuss Louise's wounds, her ecstasies, and the medical tests she underwent; all these may provide insight into the stigmatists of previous centuries, as well as those who came after Lateau.

THE AGONY AND THE ECSTASY OF LOUISE LATEAU

Louise Lateau was born in the little Belgian village of Bois-d'Haine on January 30, 1850. After the birth, Louise's mother was bedridden with an illness for months. To make matters much worse, Louise's father, Gregory Lateau, contracted smallpox and died on April 17. With her father dead and her mother so sick from childbirth that she was unable to get out of her bed, Louise's oldest sister Rosine—at the age of six—served as the primary caregiver to her mother, to her two-year-old sister Adeline, and to infant Louise, who had also contracted smallpox. To add to this nightmarish scenario, the family was quickly running out of food and ran the severe risk of starvation. Though others were aware of their plight, smallpox had made cowards of them all: no one dared visit the Lateau house to bring food out of fear of contracting the dreaded disease. Mercifully, by the end of April, a man named Francis Delalieu—who bore the name of the first stigmatist—showed up at the family door. He provided material sustenance to the impoverished family and helped nurse everyone back to health for over two years.[203]

It seems that Louise, infant though she was, somehow never forgot this man's charity at a time of crisis; in fact, she would go on to emulate him. When a cholera epidemic broke out in Belgium in 1866, the sixteen-year-old Louise beautifully and bravely echoed Delalieu's response. An 1868 article in the *Propagateur du Nord* newspaper detailed Lateau's heroic charity. It stated, "The plague was raging violently in the country, and fear had frozen everyone's hearts. Louise devoted herself to caring for the sick, and despite her mother's cautionary advice, this sixteen-year-old girl went to the bedsides of cholera patients, providing all the care that their own family members had refused to give them."[204] Imbert-Gourbeyre recounts that Louise nursed some back to health and comforted others as they lay dying. After their deaths, Louise and her sister lifted them into their coffins and personally took the coffins to the cemeteries for proper burial. Imbert-Gourbeyre underscores the fortitude of Lateau: "All this was accomplished by a child; the heroine was only sixteen years old at the time."[205] Louise was profoundly Catholic, and was fully prepared to lay down her life for her friends. Nevertheless, she survived the pandemic. After the cholera outbreak, Louise became a Third Order Franciscan, which was a fitting association: what Francis had done for the lepers, and what a Francis had done for her, Louise did for the cholera victims.

Louise became very sick the following year in late winter and early spring of 1867–1868. Her illness continually worsened and became so acute that on April 15, she was given the anointing of the sick. Within a week, however, she had completely recovered. But just a few days later, something mysterious began to happen. On Friday, April 24, 1868—when Louise was eighteen years old—blood began flowing from her left side. On the following Friday, blood flowed again from her side, and this time it was accompanied by blood flowing on the top of both her feet. The following Friday, blood flowed again. Blood came from her side, feet, and hands this time. The bleeding on Fridays became a regular occurrence. On Friday, July 17, she began to bleed from her head, which French physician Gerald Molloy described as a "coronet of bleeding points."[206] By that time, crowds began to gather around the little house on Fridays in hopes of observing Louise and her stigmatic wounds. Not knowing how to proceed, the Archbishop of Malines called in

Dr. Ferdinand Lefebvre, a University of Louvain medical professor.

When Lefebvre was first called to visit Lateau in August, he was skeptical, along with many others. He writes, "The first report of the events awakened in the public mind a feeling of distrust, and a general suspicion was aroused that it was a pious fraud, which would require but a touch of the wand of science to crumble into dust. *I do not hesitate to acknowledge that such was exactly my own feeling* when I entered for the first time the little cottage of Bois-d'Haine."[207] But after seeing Louise Lateau, Lefebvre's skepticism crumbled to dust.

Lefebvre spent considerable time examining Lateau on Fridays when her stigmata appeared and during the rest of the week when wounds did not occur. Examining her on non-Fridays, the doctor writes that the back of her hands had "oval-shaped"[208] reddish markings with a "smooth glazed look." He also notes that the palms of her hands had marks "corresponding in every respect with that on the back." He continues, "On the sole and instep of each foot the mark takes the form of a long square, with the angles rounded off, and about an inch in length." He clarifies that even though there were marks on the hands and feet, there was no blood and that the outer layer of skin "is perfectly intact." Being that Lateau suffered from a copious amount of blood during most Fridays from head wounds, Lefebvre also examined her head. He writes, "On the head, no permanent marks are visible, and save on Fridays, it is impossible to detect the points by which the blood escapes." Regarding her side wound bleeding, Lefebvre states that this was difficult to examine on non-Fridays due to modesty, but that he was able to examine her side bleeding on Fridays. In sum, though her hands and feet had some markings during the week (and her head had no markings), no blood was generally emitted during the rest of the week.

And then came Fridays. And everything changed.

Lefebvre witnessed numerous times that the stigmatic "flow of blood generally commences during the night of Thursday, or early on the Friday morning, and nearly invariably between midnight and one o'clock."[209] Though the stigmata appeared on the hands and feet and side—and usually the head—the order of wounds varied. On the occasions Lefebvre saw it, the side wound was usually the first to appear, followed by the hands, the feet, and then her head. Though there was copious bleeding from these wounds, the blood could be wiped away. Lefebvre reported that if they rubbed the hands and feet "with a linen cloth, the small triangular wound at once disappears, and the inner skin is found completely intact."

In sum, Lefebvre noted that the stigmata bore three precise characteristics: "*Spontaneity*: The blood flow occurs without the intervention of any external agent. *Periodicity*: The bleeding recurs every Friday and only appears on Fridays. *Specificity of the site*: The blood only escapes from specific points on the hands, feet, side, and head."[210]

Lefebvre was not the only physician to note this occurrence. Plenty of physicians did. For instance, on a Friday in August of 1872, Molloy traveled to Bois-d'Haine. He had been told of Lateau's story and investigated the reports firsthand. At the time, Louise was twenty-two years old. Molloy visited her, along with two dozen other people who were crammed into her room, to witness her Friday ecstasy. During that time, Louise was bleeding, and many of the visitors took out their handkerchiefs to wipe the blood from her hands to have a relic. It was then that Molloy first saw her hands.

He writes, "The nature of the stigmas was then more distinctly seen. They are oval marks of a bright-red hue, appearing on the back and palm of each hand, about the center. Speaking roughly, each stigma is about an inch in length, and somewhat more than half an inch in breadth. There is no wound, properly so called, but the blood seemed to force its way through the unbroken skin."[211] Molloy explains that this—Louise's bleeding and the visitors wiping her blood— "was repeated several times during the course of our visit."[212]

Concerning the characteristics of her side wound, Lefebvre writes, "On each of my Friday's visits . . . I have found that the blood flows from the center of the space dividing the fifth and sixth ribs, slightly below the middle of the left breast."[213] Finally, he discusses the head wound, or more accurately, *wounds*. He says the wounds differed from the others because there were "twelve or fifteen minute points, running in a circle around the forehead."[214] Dr. Gerald Molloy confirms:

> As to the coronet around the head, it consists of a large number of bleeding points which are visible on Fridays only, and which present an appearance peculiar to themselves. They cannot be conveniently examined under the hair. But on the forehead where they are from twelve to fifteen in number, they form a band about an inch wide, midway between the roots of the hair and the eyebrows. There is no permanent discoloration of the surface, no appearance of a blister, no exposure of the under skin. But, with the aid of a magnifying glass, it is possible to detect exceedingly minute punctures of the *epidermis*, through which the blood escapes.[215]

As for the amount of blood collectively lost from her hands, feet, side, and forehead, Lefebvre writes that the volume varied "considerably."[216] When Lateau first began exhibiting the wounds, some eyewitnesses assessed that she lost about a quart of blood every Friday. He puts the average Friday blood loss at eight ounces. Let's take a moment here to put that amount into perspective. It's helpful to consider that when someone donates blood, he typically donates about a pint—twice as much as Lateau was losing weekly. However, at least in America, blood donations are only allowed every eight weeks. If one were to donate a pint of blood every two weeks (the amount Lateau was losing), she would likely have a life-threatening level of anemia and a host of other problems due to the lack of red blood cells. The fact that Lateau was generally healthy as an adult is medically inexplicable for the issue of blood loss alone—to say nothing of her other conditions. Further, Lateau didn't undergo this blood loss for a few weeks or months. Except for only two Fridays, Lateau endured these Friday stigmata from age eighteen to her death at age thirty-three—the same age as Jesus when he died on the cross.

Lefebvre also addresses Lateau's suffering from her stigmata. He and other physicians who studied her point out she was a cheerful girl of beautiful disposition who never—literally, never—complained about her wounds. Nevertheless, the doctors generally agree that she suffered terribly.[217] Lefebvre writes, "In conclusion, it is to be noted that the stigmata are the seat of considerable pain. The great reticence of Louise will not allow us to appreciate exactly its intensity and nature: but, studying (at other times than the ecstasy) the play of her countenance, her attitude and whole movements, I am convinced that she must suffer severely."[218]

In addition to his report on the stigmatic wounds, Lefebvre also gives considerable attention to Louise's ecstasies. He explains that her Friday ecstasies began at about 8 a.m. and lasted "nine to twelve hours."[219] During these episodes, true to the very nature of ecstasy, she was completely unaware of her earthly surroundings. He explains that though the ecstasies began around 8 a.m., they didn't always start at that exact moment; thus, Louise might be sewing, speaking with her sister, or praying the rosary when they suddenly began. Lefebvre writes, "Suddenly her glance becomes transfixed, as by a lightning stroke; her eyes, rivetted to immoveable, are raised toward heaven—the ecstasy has commenced."[220] During most of the duration of the ecstasy, Louise sits at her chair "motionless as a statue."[221] Her eyes gaze upward and toward her right. He notes, "The whole figure of the young girl is one of profound absorbed reflection; she seems as though lost in the contemplation of some distant object."[222] The expressions and emotions on her face dramatically change throughout the ecstasy. She goes from "a beatific smile" to "an expression of deep terror" as tears drip down her face; other times her "eyes move as though following some invisible procession."[223] After this, she gets up from her chair and stands on her tiptoes, seemingly awaiting something. She mouths words quickly but inaudibly.

Lefebvre describes Lateau as plain-looking, but during the ecstasy, her face "is transfigured and lighted up with almost angelic beauty."[224] Nearly halfway into the ecstasy, he writes, Louise drops to her knees with hands folded, with her "face presenting an ever-deepening expression of the most profound contemplation."[225] An hour and a half later, her body goes into a cruciform position: her arms are outstretched to her sides, and her left foot is placed on top of her right foot. She remains in this position for two hours.

"The ecstasy terminates in a most appalling manner: the arms fall nerveless at her side, the head sinks upon the chest, the eyes close, the nose becomes pinched, the face is deadly pale and covered with a cold sweat, the hands are like ice, the pulse absolutely imperceptible, and the death rattle is heard in the throat."[226] This period lasts about a quarter of an hour, shortly after which the ecstasy concludes.

Lefebvre writes that during her ecstasies, "the functions of the senses are suspended."[227] Her eyes simply do not function in a medically-explainable way, remaining unchanging even when light is shined into them. For nine to twelve hours, her "eyes, immersed in their distant contemplation, are lost to things of earth."[228] Further, she hears nothing around her. In all his tests of her hearing, the physician found it impossible to disturb her or cause her to react: "Many times a person placed behind her has unexpectedly shouted violently in her ear, and never has she indicated her perception of it by the slightest start or tremor."[229]

When we read about some of the tests that Lefebvre describes—such as pricking her in the face with pins, shocking her with electromagnetic batteries, putting ammonia directly under her nose, and worse—anyone with a sense of pathos will feel sadness that he required these tests to illustrate the supernatural nature of Lateau's stigmata and ecstasy. Nevertheless, he did perform them. His defense in doing so was he was "thoroughly convinced . . . of the complete insensibility of the ecstatic, to the pain they would otherwise have caused her."[230] And lest we doubt these experiments' sincerity, accuracy, or completeness, we should remember that about one hundred doctors assisted Lefebvre in his experiments. We should also note that, during the course of his examinations, Lefebvre sent out many invitations to medical professors at the universities of Liege, Ghent, and

Brussels to observe Lateau. With one exception, they all turned him down. The free-thinkers simply mocked Lateau as a fraud without even visiting her.[231] He writes, nevertheless, "Neither myself, nor any of the other doctors, or other witnesses of these tests, have ever once been able to detect the slightest indication of sensibility, or indeed of the least muscular contraction."[232]

Lefebvre concludes that while "strangers to her life" might offer doubt, ridicule, and accusations of fraud, "no one with the slightest knowledge of Louise Lateau has suspected her for a single moment of a deception."[233] This is a crucial point. The account of her care for the cholera victims defines Lateau's character well. Her biographers point out that Lateau attended Mass daily and was a holy, cheerful, charitable person and a diligent seamstress worker. As we'll see, she had her share of shameless and cruel critics, but those who met her seem to have found it impossible to dislike her. A few months after Louise's stigmata began, the Archbishop of Malines had a long discussion with Lateau to determine her character. After the meeting, the archbishop turned to her parish priest and assured him, "Be at peace, you have a saint in your parish."[234] This was a common consensus not only of prelates but of doctors and many of her visitors, including those who were very biased against Louise and her Catholic faith.

Of course, there were also those who believed in both the science of medicine and the science of mystical theology—and this brings us to the person of Dr. Imbert-Gourbeyre. On October 23, 1868, the French doctor visited Louise to observe her reported stigmata. What he saw that day would forever influence his life and the way that people around the world viewed the stigmata.

DR. ANTOINE IMBERT-GOURBEYRE

Imbert-Gourbeyre was a gifted physician and a polymath within the medical field; he conducted groundbreaking research on topics including typhoid fever, dermatology, and cardiology. Moreover, his life and writings illustrate a man of great compassion and empathy. One of the things that made him exceptional was his quest for truth, which is not always easy within the medical field. Aristotle notes that truth is "the mind's conformity with reality," but within science and medicine, it is clear that fame, popularity, and acceptance of one's peers prove to form a virus that is highly resistant to truth.

When Imbert-Gourbeyre began to report about his findings of Lateau's stigmata (coupled with his belief in the apparitions of the Immaculate Conception at Lourdes and La-Salette), he was largely shunned by the medical community. In Imbert-Gourbeyre's time, Enlightenment thinking was dominant in the European scientific and medical community. Among the "free-thinking" (atheist) intelligentsia, the Catholic religion was often seen as an anachronistic nuisance—an uninvited obstacle to scientific progress. The last thing the free-thinkers wanted was a widespread discussion of the wounds of Christ that somehow appeared on the bodies of devout Catholics, especially from an accomplished physician who lent medical and scientific credibility not only to contemporary stigmatists, but to hundreds of stigmatists over the centuries. Imbert-Gourbeyre must have known that his scientific defense of the stigmata was kicking a hornet's nest, but—dedicating his book to the Lord Jesus crucified—he happily wrote extensively about the stigmata, despite the inevitable scorn he received from many of his peers.

Imbert-Gourbeyre conducted extensive scientific research on the stigmatists and simply reporting his findings, but such findings were strictly forbidden (in modern times, we might use the word "canceled") in Enlightenment Europe. Sadly, Imbert-Gourbeyre's treatment by the medical community paralleled a contemporary physician who was also blacklisted: Ignaz Semmelweis.

Born into a large Catholic family in modern-day-Budapest just four months after Imbert-Gourbeyre in 1818, Semmelweis received his degree in medicine in 1844. His great interest was in obstetrics, and Semmelweis was alarmed at the fact that postpartum women were commonly dying of puerperal fever in maternity hospitals, yet—curiously—their chances of dying of the same sickness were considerably lower elsewhere, even in the streets of the city. Motivated by a deep compassion and empathy, Semmelweis tirelessly researched the cause. Through cleanliness practices, scientific observation, and precise record-keeping, Semmelweis discovered—and enacted—a way to nearly eliminate postpartum mortality entirely. He identified the problem: obstetricians were not washing their hands prior to delivering babies.[235] He thus devised a hand-washing soap for physicians to use prior to delivery. Under his direction at a maternity hospital in Vienna, the incidents of "fatal puerperal fever" immediately dropped by almost 90 percent.[236]

Semmelweis saved so many lives that he was dubbed the "Savior of Mothers." Tragically, his colleagues refused to adopt Semmelweis's procedures; instead, they responded with indifference or even hatred. These were men who did not like being questioned. In 1861, Semmelweis issued a 524-page book detailing his findings, yet the medical community ignored, shunned, and mocked him for it. They simply could not bring themselves to believe that Semmelweis could be right and the rest of the medical community wrong. Semmelweis was fired from his post, yet the attacks on him continued. The emotional effects on Semmelweis were devastating.[237] In 1865, he was committed to a mental institution, where he was promptly beaten by a guard and put into a straitjacket. He died two weeks after his arrival, likely from the infected wounds he sustained from that beating.[238]

Though he didn't live to see it, the work of Semmelweis saved not hundreds, but millions of lives. As Newton might have phrased it, Louis Pasteur and Joseph Lister stood on the giant shoulders of Semmelweis to see farther. Biographer William J. Sinclair provides an excellent yet heartbreaking summary of the tremendous contribution of Semmelweis to mankind, along with the shameful way he was treated:

> Many men in all generations have looked into nature with their natural vision undimmed by the teaching of pedants: many men have been endowed with clear intellects and hearts full of love for their fellow men, with the enthusiasm of humanity, and they have been enabled to achieve some signal service for the human race in their day and generation; but in the whole history of medicine there is only one Semmelweis in the magnitude of his services to mankind, and in the depth of his sufferings from contemporary jealous stupidity and ingratitude.[239]

To underscore the point: Semmelweis was simply reporting what he saw, and he was hated for seeing it. Though Semmelweis was more harshly treated than Imbert-Gourbeyre, the latter nevertheless endured criticism and mockery—for seeing something he wasn't supposed to see: the mystical stigmata.

Imbert-Gourbeyre's encounter with Lateau had a profound effect on his life and his work. He was so intrigued by

Lateau that he wrote a lengthy biography about her and her stigmata. But that was only the beginning. Lateau's case fascinated him so much that he spent two decades researching and writing a multi-volume biography of all reported stigmatists in history. In the 1894 edition of his book, he came back with a definitive number of stigmatists: three hundred and twenty-one—of whom forty-one were men, and two hundred and eighty were women. He states that his main goal for the book was to "scientifically defend the miracle of stigmatization."[240]

Imbert-Gourbeyre's book about Lateau was published in 1873 (about four years after Lefebvre's original book) and explains his studies and experiments on Lateau.[241] The book deserves to be read in full because it provides extensive detail that shines a great light not only on her stigmata and ecstasies but on the person of Louise Lateau. For that matter, his book offers an exacting description of both stigmata and ecstasy; this volume—as well as subsequent volumes—forms a comprehensive apologetic for the miraculous nature of the stigmata. And even beyond all that, his volumes allow for a deeper understanding of the nature of miracles themselves. Indeed, some of the writings of Antoine Imbert-Gourbeyre should be required reading for every student of Catholic mystical theology. Sadly, aside from a few translated passages from the original French contained in books about the stigmata, his works have never been formally translated into English. In any case, though time and space do not allow a more complete treatment of his writing, we will focus on several of his most important insights that build upon Lefebvre's observations.

Gourbeyre offered broad confirmations of Lefebvre's medical research; in fact, he did many of the same tests on the stigmata—as did other physicians. One of the tests is particularly noteworthy. Some speculated that Lateau was putting something on her hands and feet to produce blisters, so the following test was conducted. Over four days and nights, "Louise was fitted with perfectly fitting leather gloves that conformed closely to her hands, with the fingers, backs, and palms snugly fitting as if molded. These gloves were tightened around the wrists using cords passed through loops, and the knots were sealed. Each day, these seals were inspected. Despite wearing these gloves, blisters formed, and blood flowed abundantly."[242]

But as much as Gourbeyre was intrigued by the medically inexplicable stigmata themselves, he seems even more fascinated by Lateau's medically inexplicable ecstasies—and the events that occurred within them. For instance, during her ecstasies, she simultaneously experienced her pulse rise to 130 beats per minute, her breathing slowed by half, and her arms and legs became "as cold as marble."[243] Gourbeyre writes, "No one in the world can, for several consecutive hours, cause themselves such a considerable increase in pulse rate, a significant drop in temperature, and a reduction by half in the number of respiratory acts. Note also the remarkable fact of the coinciding of the reduction in respiration with the increase in pulse rate, which goes against all the rules of pathological physiology."[244] He further noted that, over three hours of the ecstasy, her body moved in a way "which defies all the laws of gravity."[245] In addition, there is the fact that during her ecstasies, she had no sensory awareness. Lefebvre discussed this in detail, and Gourbeyre confirms it, writing: "Louise, as evidenced by the investigation and my own experiments, has always resisted all external agents during ecstasy, allowing herself to be pinched, pricked, cauterized, burned, and electrified without showing the slightest sensitivity."[246] Again, beyond the tragedy of the fact that Louise was subject to these sorts of tests by many doctors, it is clear that she did—in fact—undergo these tests.

Gourbeyre asked her what she saw during her ecstasies, and she explained, "Very often, I see the holy Virgin, our Lord, I see lights. I have seen our Lord on Calvary several times and various scenes of the passion. Today, I saw bright lights and a cross. . . . I have often seen St. Francis of Assisi."[247]

Gourbeyre also references another unique ability of Lateau's that is easy to explain through mystical theology but very difficult to explain through medicine: in her ecstasies, she could distinguish between *ordinary objects* and *sacraments or sacramentals.* For instance, Lateau could spiritually sense the Real Presence—the body, blood, soul, and divinity of Jesus in the Eucharist. In the state of ecstasy, she was repeatedly able to distinguish between consecrated and unconsecrated hosts. (As we will see in the following chapter, this uncommon trait was a common ability among the stigmatists.) Beyond that, she could distinguish between otherwise identical blessed and unblessed items.[248]

In January of 1869, a group of doctors—including at least one free-thinking Dr. Delcroix—gathered to perform tests on Louise in her state of ecstasy to see if this rumored ability of Lateau's were legitimate. Gourbeyre recounts, "During a long examination session, these gentlemen repeatedly presented Louise with blessed and non-blessed objects, such as medals, crosses, and rosaries."[249] However, she was not told which objects were blessed and which were not, and it would be medically inexplicable to distinguish between them with the naked eye. For instance, seeing a rosary for the first time, a Catholic woman might observe that a rosary was "blue" or "pretty," but she would have no natural way of discerning whether the rosary were blessed. Nevertheless, when blessed items were put before Louise, she smiled; when unblessed items were held before her, she ignored them. The free-thinking Delcroix was so amazed by Lateau's identification that he soon converted to the Catholic faith, dying shortly after that in the arms of the Church.[250]

The news of this discerning power of Lateau's quickly spread, but the free-thinkers broadly doubted, so they assembled another group of doctors to run tests. The result was the same, so the tests became even trickier. For example, an unblessed image of the crucified Jesus was placed on Louise's lips, and she gave no response. A priest blessed the same picture behind her back and represented the picture to her, and she smiled. The Count of Beaufort visited Louise and presented her with another test. He held his blessed wedding ring before her face, and she smiled; he then placed an unblessed ring, and she had no response.[251] Gourbeyre observes, "It is curious that it was the doctors, greatly divided on the question of the supernatural, who took the initiative for all these experiments. They were conducted with the highest scientific rigor; tests and counter-tests, nothing was lacking. It is therefore impossible to have the slightest doubt about their validity. Since that time, they have been multiplied in all forms; they even went to the point of excess, as if Louise were a real experimental machine."[252]

Gourbeyre estimates that over one thousand such tests were presented to Lateau (many of which were conducted by those hostile to both Lateau and hateful to the Catholic Church), and in all but two cases Lateau was able to identify correctly.[253] Mathematically, the accuracy of such discernment is more impressive than selecting *one* correct atom hidden *somewhere* in the universe.

Along with the power to discern sacraments and sacramentals, Louise also had the power to understand foreign languages in prayer. In her entire life, Louise had perhaps five months of formal schooling; outside her ecstasies, Louise knew only the French language. Yet somehow, she recognized prayers in foreign languages, including Latin, English, Flemish, German, and Greek. When she heard prayers in these languages during her ecstasies, she would smile with ebullience and profound joy. Yet, when someone read Homer's *Iliad* in Greek, she gave no response whatsoever.[254]

These experiments were both well-documented and widely known. By 1873, Lateau had been examined by at least three hundred doctors and visited by thousands of men and women of both religious and irreligious perspectives. By the time Gourbeyre published his book, even those who were openly hostile to the Catholic faith had largely abandoned their "fraud" thesis, a narrative that they had once held so dearly. As an article in the *Journal of Religious History* points out, "Research on the Belgian liberal newspapers in fact suggests a chronological evolution in the way Louise is presented. In the first phase, 1869–1873, she is presented as a 'fraud,' while from 1874 to 1875 onwards she is described as 'ill.'"[255] This diagnosis of Lateau became the popular narrative among the rationalist critics—the vast majority of whom had never set foot in Bois-d'Haine.

An article in the May 18, 1879 edition of *The New York Times* states, "There seems to be no reason for supposing that there was any deceit on the part of Louise Lateau herself, though that she was self-deceived no one can reasonably doubt. Of course, many in Belgium, especially the more ignorant and superstitious, (including large numbers of the clergy and of religious orders of men and women,) believed that her ecstasies were miraculous, and no doubt she believed them herself. But none of the circumstances observed in her case, or related by her, were such as the physiologist would find any difficulty in accepting or explaining."[256] The fact that the article does not refer to a single physician who was confounded—not to mention *converted*—by Lateau is staggering. There is a mountain of falsehood in this article that can easily be refuted by anyone who has read this chapter thus far. Still, the article also exposes an utter disdain for anyone who professes the Catholic faith—writing them off as simply "ignorant and superstitious."

Near the end of his book, Gourbeyre encapsulates the scene of the Lateau family at Bois-d'Haine in 1873:

> There are no posters, advertisements, or exhibitions. They do not charge five francs at the door. The ecstatic lives in poverty with her family, avoiding wealth, noise, and splendor along with her family. However, for the past five years, people from Belgium have flocked to her cottage. They have come from France, Germany, England, and elsewhere. This simple daughter of the people has received visits from the entire Belgian episcopate. . . . The sick in body and soul have come in crowds. Louise has been visited by men of all ranks and conditions: men of the military, men of science, men of state. People quarrel for a few drops of her blood every Friday; they have faith in the prayers of the ecstatic. I saw the queen of the Belgians send one of her ladies-in-waiting to Bois-d'Haine to ask Louise to pray for the dying crown prince. When you enter the humble dwelling, you have no doubt about the truthfulness and nature of the facts; you simply admire, pray, and venerate.[257]

This same scene endured with little change until Lateau's death ten years later. By the time she died, she had been one of the most medically and psychologically-examined persons in history. She shed light on the stigmata for the whole world to see, or more accurately, God shed light on the wounds of his stigmata in the body of Louise Lateau for the world to see. Whether the rationalists liked it or not, "stigmata" had entered the lexicon of common parlance.

CANONIZED STIGMATISTS OF THE TWENTIETH CENTURY

After giving considerable attention to Louise Lateau, we must highlight the fact that she is not—at least as of this writing—canonized, declared blessed, or even venerable. Of course, we can certainly hope and pray that—if it is the holy will of God—she is eventually declared a saint. The fact that fourteen decades have passed since her death in 1883 does not indicate that she will never be canonized, even if three stigmatists who lived and died in the twentieth century have been canonized already. The firstborn among them, St. Gemma Galgani (whom we referenced in the previous chapter), was five years old when Louise Lateau died. Gemma lived a very short life and only survived into the early years of the century. The second was not only a man—which was rare among the stigmatists—but also a priest, St. Padre Pio. The third among them was both born and died early in the twentieth century. Her baptism name was Helen.

Before we begin the discussion of the stigmatists of the twentieth century, let's examine the twentieth century itself, which was the most violent of centuries. Tens of millions of people—both soldiers and civilians—died in two world wars. And if the twentieth century was the devil's playground, the devil had new toys. World War I introduced the machine gun, which racked up casualties by the second.

World War II introduced the atomic bomb. Also new was the use of nerve gas to terrorize the innocents around the globe. One wonders if the devil himself could have conducted more murderous regimes than Lenin and Stalin in Russia, Hitler in Germany, Mao Tse-tung in China, Ho Chi Minh in Vietnam, Idi Amin in Uganda, Kim Il-Sung followed by Kim Jong Il in North Korea, and Fidel Castro in Cuba. The list goes on. It provides a chilling commentary about the widespread demonic violence of the twentieth century that most Westerners have long forgotten the name Pol Pot, the leader of the Communist Party who gleefully murdered so many Cambodians that well over one million innocents were thrown into mass graves, so vast and mind-numbing was the horror of the twentieth century, truly a well-documented antithesis of the virtue of mercy.

In the midst of this unspeakable chaos, however, we must remember that God sends those men and women—those saints—who are most needed at the time. St. Faustina Kowalska (1905–1938), who would make known to the world the message of Divine Mercy, confirms that principle. In his divine Providence, God sent her into a world on the eve of unspeakable mercilessness. What is even more fitting is that she was born in Poland, where World War II began with Hitler's invasion. The Catholic biographer J.K. Huysmans writes, "All through the ages there have been found saints willing to pay, by their sufferings, the ransom for the sins and faults of others."[258] Faustina's *Diary* evidences a woman who was heroically willing to do just that.

Faustina (Helen Kowalska) explains that when she was only seven years old, "I heard God's voice in my soul."[259] This would only be the first of many times that Helen heard the voice of God. When she was eighteen, Helen desperately appealed to her parents to permit her to enter the convent, but her parents refused. After this, Helen's thoughts wandered away from thoughts of the religious life to more worldly pursuits and entertainment. During a dance, Jesus appeared to her and asked, "How long shall I put up with you and how long will you keep putting Me off?"[260] Rushing to the nearby Cathedral of St. Stanislaus Kostka, Helen fell down in adoration of the Eucharist, and pleaded with Jesus for instructions on how to proceed in following him. She heard a voice: "Go at once to Warsaw; you will enter a convent there."[261]

Soon afterward, Helen joined the Sisters of Our Lady of Mercy and, in 1926, took the name "Sr. Mary Faustina of the Most Blessed Sacrament." Five years later, Jesus appeared to Faustina with a special request. In her diary, she recounts,

> In the evening, when I was in my cell, I saw the Lord Jesus clothed in a white garment. One hand [was] raised in the gesture of blessing, the other was touching the garment at the breast. From beneath the garment, slightly drawn aside at the breast, there were emanating two large rays, one red, the other pale. In silence I kept my gaze fixed on the Lord; my soul was struck with awe, but also with great joy.
>
> After a while, Jesus said to me, "Paint an image according to the pattern you see, with the signature: Jesus, I trust in you. I desire that this image be venerated, first in your chapel, and [then] throughout the world. I promise that the soul that will venerate this image will not perish. I also promise victory over [its] enemies already here on earth, especially at the hour of death. I myself will defend it as my own glory."[262]

The Divine Mercy painting is the fulfillment of that request, and today, reproductions of the image adorn churches and homes on all the continents of earth.

Though Faustina was widely known before her canonization in the latter half of the twentieth century, her canonization by Pope St. John Paul II magnified the message of Jesus' unfathomable mercy through her. This fulfilled and continues to fulfill Jesus' words to her, who had chosen her, as he said, "to make known to souls the great mercy that I have for them, and to exhort them to trust in the bottomless depth of my mercy."[263] He continued, "I am sending you with my mercy to the people of the whole world. I do not want to punish aching mankind, but I desire to heal it, pressing it to my merciful heart. . . . You are the secretary of my mercy; I have chosen you for that office in this life and the next life."[264]

What even many Catholics who have a great devotion to St. Faustina do not know, however, is that she suffered the wounds of the Passion in invisible stigmata. She explains in her diary, "When I experienced these sufferings for the first time, it was like this: after the annual vows, on a certain day, during prayer, I saw a great brilliance and, issuing from the brilliance, rays which completely enveloped me. Then suddenly, I felt a terrible pain in my hands, my feet and my side and the thorns of the crown of thorns. I experienced these sufferings during holy Mass on Friday, but this was only for a brief moment. This was repeated for several Fridays."[265] In the years that followed, Sr. Faustina experienced stigmatic pains numerous times. Her description of them in September of 1936 provides great insight into the reason for the stigmata itself: suffering for others. She writes,

> During holy Mass one Friday, I felt myself pierced by the same sufferings, and this has been repeated on every Friday and sometimes when I meet a soul that is not in the state of grace. Although this is infrequent, and the suffering lasts a very short time, still it is terrible, and I would not be able to bear it without a special grace from God. There is no outward indication of these sufferings. What will come later, I do not know. All this, for the sake of souls.[266]

Later in her diary, she writes, "Today, for a short while, I experienced the pain of the crown of thorns. I was praying for a certain soul before the Blessed Sacrament at the time. In an instant, I felt such a violent pain that my head dropped onto the altar rail. Although this moment was very brief, it was very painful."[267] As Jesus endured the Passion and Crucifixion for the sake of sinners, Faustina was willing to shoulder the burden of the sins of others for the sake of their souls.

This is the message of Jesus' passion. This is the message of mercy. This is the message of the stigmata. To borrow the words of the Divine Mercy chaplet, Faustina endured the mystical stigmata "for the sake of his sorrowful passion." Like Catherine of Siena and Lucy of Narni, Faustina suffered bloodless stigmata. Perhaps this was to illustrate that one is not required to shed blood to endure suffering for others. The vast majority of empathetic suffering does not involve the shedding of blood—and it is a dangerous and erroneous proposition that suggests otherwise. Of course, the reason for invisibility could simply lie in humility, but then, every saint is humble. Faustina, however, had a particular devotion to the practice of holy silence. To consider only a few brief extracts from her *Diary:*

> In the sufferings of soul or body, I try to keep silence, for then my spirit gains the strength that flows from the Passion of Jesus. I have ever before my eyes his sorrowful face, abused and disfigured, his divine heart pierced by our sins and especially by the ingratitude of chosen souls.[268]

> In the silence of my heart I kept saying to myself, "O Christ, may delights, honor and glory be yours, and suffering be mine. I will not lag one step behind as I follow you, though thorns wound my feet."[269]

> O my Jesus, you alone know the longings and the sufferings of my heart. I am glad I can suffer for you, however little. When I feel that the suffering is more than I can bear, I take refuge in the Lord in the Blessed Sacrament, and I speak to him with profound silence.[270]

Not only did Faustina strive to suffer in silence, but silence itself became her special share in the passion of the Lord, as she was held in derision by those who could not understand it.* Indeed, Sr. Faustina only mentioned her pain at her spiritual adviser's counsel to write about it; otherwise,

* Cf. John 19:9–11. See, for example, *Diary of St. Faustina*, no. 126: "I resolved to bear everything in silence and to give no explanations when I was questioned. Some were irritated by my silence, especially those who were more curious. Others, who reflected more deeply, said, 'Sister Faustina must be very close to God if she has the strength to bear so much suffering.' It was as if I were facing two groups of judges. I strove after interior and exterior silence. I said nothing about myself, even though I was questioned directly by some sisters. My lips were sealed. I suffered like a dove, without complaint. But some sisters seemed to find pleasure in vexing me in whatever way they could. My patience irritated them. But God gave me so much inner strength that I endured it calmly."

the world may have never known about her stigmata at all. That is a particularly intriguing speculation, not only as it applies to Faustina but to the virtually unknown holy men and women of Christendom who may have been granted invisible stigmata as well.

Like Louise Lateau and Catherine of Siena, Faustina died at age thirty-three. The "Secretary of Mercy" could now do her work—as Jesus had promised—in heaven. And she needed to pray very hard in the presence of God, because eleven months after she died, Adolf Hitler rolled his tanks into her native Poland to begin World War II.

Although Faustina's stigmata would be virtually unknown before her death, there was a stigmatist in Italy whose wounds were widely known during his lifetime: Padre Pio. Baptized—so fittingly as it turned out—with the named Francesco, the future Padre Pio was born into a family of seven children (two of whom died in infancy). He was ordained as a priest at the age of twenty-three, and his stigmata began shortly after that in various stages.[271] Similarly to St. Gertrude the Great, St. Clare of Montefalco, and St. Catherine of Siena, in August of 1918, Padre Pio received the heart stigma. Though his stigmata had already manifested outward signs temporarily on earlier occasions, the "permanent stigmata" began on September 20, 1918.[272] And whether it be coincidence or Providence, on that same day—September 20, 1918—a battle took place in the hometown of Jesus. In the closing days of World War I, British and Ottoman forces clashed at the Battle of Nazareth. At the very moment that the earthly home of the Prince of Peace was under siege, God manifested the wounds of the Passion in his priestly representative on earth. We still need the wounds of God to save us men and women from our sins; the phenomenon of stigmata is physical evidence of that inescapable reality.

As for Padre Pio's stigmata, they were similar in some respects to those of other stigmatists: he bore wounds on his hands, feet, and side. But they were also different from most other stigmata in several ways. One difference was its duration: whereas many stigmatists only bore the five wounds on Fridays, Padre Pio bore them constantly. In fact, not only were his wounds present seven days a week, but his wounds endured for fifty years. That's a striking fact, even for a stigmatist, due to sheer blood loss alone. His side wound was witnessed to lose eight ounces of blood a day.[273] There were other medical peculiarities, including the fact that, as one of his physicians confirmed in his official report, Padre Pio's body temperature would sometimes reach one hundred and twenty degrees.[274] However, the most unique aspect of Padre Pio's stigmata was not the wounds but the man who bore them. As far as we know, no other priest has ever borne the stigmata. This created some dilemmas for his superiors.

A significant percentage of blessed and canonized stigmatists lived quiet lives in secluded religious communities; thus, they were not under much, if any, public scrutiny. Many of them never saw "the public" after receiving the stigmata. There may be a widespread myth among non-Catholics that the stigmata are simply a hoax conducted to raise money for the Catholic Church, but the aggregate evidence over the past eight centuries confirms the opposite case. Church officials have almost always been extremely cautious and guarded about the stigmata. In overwhelming measure, ecclesiastics have simply preferred not to discuss the stigmata. But in the case of a priest, keeping silent was a much different matter. Padre Pio's superiors insisted that his stigmata be hidden as much as possible, but that was not an easy thing to accomplish. How do you hide the stigmata in a priest's hands when he raises the Eucharist? Padre Pio himself was initially embarrassed to display his wounds, so he wore fingerless gloves, raising intrigue among the faithful about what was beneath those gloves.

Because he was so popular, his superiors recommended he say a very early Mass, which was intended to limit the size of his congregation; however, this increased his popularity, and people started coming in droves to these early liturgies.[275] He also heard confessions, sometimes for sixteen hours a day.[276] He seemed to combine St. Francis of Assisi and St. John Vianney. How, precisely, do you prevent the Catholic faithful from flocking to such a person—even though the person desperately eschews celebrity?

Various rumors spread about Padre Pio and the notion that he was somehow faking his stigmata (a common theme in a rationalist age, so embarrassed at the thought of miracles). For all his greatness, Pope Pius XI made an ill-informed decision in 1931 to suppress Padre Pio's priestly ministry. A formal decree from Rome stated, "Padre Pio da Pietrelcina is deprived of any exercise of ministry with the sole exception of celebrating holy Mass, but inside the walls of the convent, in the chapel privately, and not in public."[277] When Pope Pius realized that his decision was a mistake—admitting that the information communicated to him had been faulty—he began gradually to reinstate Padre Pio's priestly ministry. Still, his powers were only fully restored in 1941, during the pontificate of Pope Pius XII.[278] Though it must have caused him tremendous anguish, Padre Pio was obedient to his superiors, especially to the reigning pontiffs.[279] Padre Pio died on September 23, 1968, at the age of eighty-one. He had such a profound influence that 100,000 people attended his funeral.

Next to Francis of Assisi, Padre Pio is perhaps the most widely-remembered and widely-loved stigmatist among Catholics today. One of the reasons for that is straightforward: he lived during our lifetime or the lifetime of our parents. Many Catholics still alive today have personally met him or at least attended Mass that was said by him. Though Pope John Paul II did not mention the "stigmata" during his canonization for Padre Pio, he seemed to allude to it, stating, "Throughout his life, he always sought greater conformity with the Crucified, since he was very conscious of having been called to collaborate in a special way in the work of redemption. His holiness cannot be understood without this constant reference to the cross."[280] The same could be said of every blessed and canonized stigmatist.

BLESSEDS, VENERABLES, SERVANTS, & HONORABLE MENTIONS

As of yet, there have only been three canonized stigmatists who lived and died in the twentieth century, but others have been declared Servants of God, Venerable, and Blessed. There are also other reported stigmatists of significant interest.

Sr. Josefa Menendez (1890–1923) became a sister of the Society of the Sacred Heart at age twenty-nine. In 1920, she began to experience stigmatic pains, including those of the cross on her shoulder and the crown of thorns on her head. She accepted her pain out of great love for Jesus, as well as for sinners, whom she ardently desired to help bring back to the Catholic Church.[281] As with many mystical stigmatists, Jesus appeared to Josefa many times. On one such occasion, Jesus explained something that caused him great pain: the sins of priests.

"Innumerable are the sins committed, and innumerable the souls that are damned," he said. "But what wounds my Heart above measure is the sinfulness of those that are consecrated to me. . . . Poor, poor soul! If he but realized the agony he is preparing for himself for all eternity."[282] Sr. Josefa's stigmatic suffering was not in vain. Jesus assured her that it brought souls back to him. Jesus said, "Josefa . . . let me tell you of my joy: those three souls that I had entrusted to you have come back to me."[283] Josefa—like Faustina, Louise Lateau, and Catherine of Siena—died at the same age our Lord did.

Servant of God Therese Neumann (1898–1962) was born in Bavaria on Good Friday of 1898 into a materially poor Catholic family that would eventually welcome ten more children.[284] She began receiving visions at a young age. She recounts, "At my First Communion, when the priest (Fr. Ebel) was distributing the Sacred Host to me, I saw not the host, not the priest, but the glorified child Jesus; I saw this, however, at that time, not as something extraordinary; I thought that this was what everyone experienced on this occasion."[285] This was only the beginning of many mystical experiences.

As we have seen, many future stigmatists endure terrible illnesses and pain prior to their receptions of the stigmata. Therese was no different in that regard. When she was nineteen years old, she was helping extinguish a fire at a neighbor's farm when her spine was twisted out of position, eventually leaving her paralyzed. This condition wreaked further havoc on her body: within a year, she gradually went blind. Though the family and physicians did all they could to treat her condition, neither her paralysis nor blindness improved.[286] But through it all, Therese maintained a heroically sweet disposition and acceptance. When her father returned home from World War I, he brought his daughter a holy card of Sr. Thérèse of Lisieux that she treasured. She developed a deep devotion to the Little Flower, who had not yet been canonized or beatified.

That was all about to change, and so was Therese Neumann's health.

On April 29, 1923, Sr. Thérèse of Lisieux was beatified in Rome by Pope Pius XI, making her Bl. Thérèse of Lisieux. On that same day, Therese Neumann was saying the prayer of Thérèse of Lisieux to the Child Jesus. She fell asleep and "dreamed that someone was touching her pillow."[287] When she awoke, her sight was fully restored, although she was still paralyzed.

Not long after, on May 17, 1925, Thérèse was canonized by Pope Pius XI. Having promised, "I will spend my heaven in doing good upon earth," the new saint didn't waste any time. By the spring of 1925, Therese Neumann had suffered from paralysis for seven years, and her condition had grown worse. Her left foot had been worn down to the bone and had developed such a severe infection that the physician considered amputation. But she had an idea: she owned a rose petal that had been touched to a relic of Thérèse of Lisieux, and she asked her sister to place that petal in her foot's bandage.

On May 17, reminiscent of Jesus' cure of the paralytic recounted in John 5:6, Therese heard a voice asking if she wanted to be healed. She answered, "I want anything and everything that comes from God."[288] And the voice responded, "Today you may have another little joy. You can sit up; try it at once, I'll help you."[289] The very same day—perhaps the exact moment—that Thérèse of Lisieux was formally recognized as a saint by the universal Church, Therese's foot was fully healed, her legs were straightened, and she rose to walk around the room. This is a medically documented, medically inexplicable, complete recovery.

Less than one year later, in 1926, Therese Neumann received the five main wounds of the stigmata on Good Friday at the age of twenty-eight. Much like Louise Lateau, she was seen by many physicians who could not explain her wounds through the lens of medical science. Fr. Thurston notes, "With regard to the fact of the bleeding wound-marks in hands, feet and side of which we read in the accounts of Theresa Neumann and a multitude of others, there cannot be a shadow of doubt. . . . Theresa has often been under observation during the whole time the ecstasy and bleeding have developed."[290] Even more specifically, multiple physicians noted that not only did wounds appear, but so did nails in the wounds. One of those reports indicated that "a sort of nail forms in the wounds and seems to consist of firm, grisly flesh; one got the impression of a forged iron nail which goes through the hand from outside to the inside, the end of which appears to have been bent round by a hammer blow."[291] A doctor from Versailles similarly noted, "On the back of the left hand I see a nail head, rectangular in shape, slightly longer than broad, in line with the hand. The rectangle it forms may be fifteen millimeters by ten; its edges are fined down and almost sharp, like those of an iron convex, rounded in a dome shape. It shows numerous planes, not defined, like those produced by the blows of a smith's hammer."[292]

During her ecstasies, Therese Neumann's wounds occurred in the order that Jesus received them. As one doctor explained,

> As a proof of the miraculous nature of these phenomena, nothing can be more convincing to a doctor than the remarkable way in which the times that Teresa Neumann's stigmata bleed correspond with the times of Our divine Lord's sufferings. Thus, her hands bleed when our Lord's hands are bound in the Garden of Gethsemani, the

> stigmata of the scourges bleed at 6 a.m. (8 a.m. Jerusalem time) when our Lord was scourged; the bleeding of the wounds on her head begins soon after as she sees the crown of thorns placed on our Lord's head; the shoulder wound bleeds during the vision of the carrying of the cross and again when our Lord is stripped of his garments; and the wounds of her hands and feet bleed profusely during the vision of the crucifixion.[293]

Therese Neumann experienced these stigmatic events weekly for the rest of her life, passing away on September 18, 1962, at the age of 64. In 2005, Bishop Gerhard Muller, now a cardinal, opened the cause for her beatification.

Venerable Marthe Robin (1902–1981) was born in a tiny village in southeastern France, the youngest of six children. Typhoid fever swept through the Robin house, leaving one of her siblings dead and Marthe deathly ill. Marthe recovered, but the effects of her illness endured for many years.[294] Though her parents were nominally Catholic—attending Mass only on Easter—Marthe had a deep love and affection for God even as a little girl, and she attended Sunday Mass with her sisters.[295] In 1918, she began to suffer terribly from an illness that lasted in its effects, such as paralysis, for years. Swelling of the brain was speculated. Whatever it was, it produced several comas and brought her to the point of death numerous times.[296]

Her parents largely ignored and resented her and her illness; meanwhile, Marthe grew closer to Mary, the Mother of God. On the Feast of the Annunciation in 1922, Marthe had a vision of the Blessed Virgin Mary.[297] By October 1927, Marthe had been in so much pain and was so sick that she felt perfectly prepared to die in the state of sanctifying grace. Marthe fell into a coma but recovered from it with some remarkable news: Thérèse of Lisieux had visited her in her comatose state and assured her that Marthe would live on to continue the mission of Thérèse on earth. This granted a powerful value to her life's suffering. Shortly after that vision, Marthe wrote something in her *Journal* that gives us a great insight into the very meaning of the stigmata: "I want to lead many, many souls to Jesus only by my love and by the total offering of my life as a sick person, not having any other will save that of my God, or rather by uniting my own will totally to that of my God."[298]

Three years later, in October of 1930, she received the mystical stigmata—invisible at first, then visible a year later. From that point forward, she manifested the wounds of the stigmata on her hands, feet, and head fairly regularly on Fridays for the rest of her life. Like Louise Lateau in Belgium, Marthe Robin and her stigmata were common knowledge in France.[299] Though illness and paralysis confined her, one of her biographers notes that "in the course of some fifty years this gravely ill woman received over one hundred thousand people in her room."[300] From her bedroom, Robin founded an organization called the Foyers of Charity, and felt called to write about God's mercy in unmerciful times. Her message was contained in her words, *"The mercy of God surpasses all his works, and he performs his greatest masterpieces of love in the midst of the greatest human misery."*[301]

During Marthe Robin's beatification proceedings, "fifty people" testified that they "had seen blood flowing from Marthe's wounds."[302] Likely hundreds more people would have been willing and able to testify. Her funeral Mass was concelebrated by more than 200 priests and 6,000 communicants.[303] She was declared venerable by Pope Francis in 2014.

Bl. Alexandrina da Costa (1904–1955) was born in Balazar, Portugal. On Holy Saturday of 1918, one year after Our

Lady of Fátima had appeared to the shepherd children in that country, Alexandrina was sewing dresses with her sister and a friend for Easter Mass the next day. Suddenly, three drunken men attempted to burst into the living room with the intention of raping the young women. To protect herself, Alexandrina jumped out the second-story window and fell twelve feet to the ground—badly damaging her spine in the process.[304] Though the extent of her injuries was not immediately exhibited, spinal damage would leave her paralyzed for the rest of her life. Confined to her bed, Alexandrina achieved lofty holiness through closeness to Jesus and Mary. Her writing also evidences a devotion to Thérèse of Lisieux.[305] On October 3, 1938—the feast day of Thérèse of Lisieux—Alexandrina received the stigmata. Her weekly stigmatic pains resembled those of Jesus' passion.

As we have seen, all stigmata are remarkable, but not always for the same reasons. Alexandrina received the stigmata after she had been paralyzed for thirteen years, which made ecstasies even more difficult to explain from a medical perspective. And hers was an ecstasy much like Louise Lateau's, insofar as her body imitated the events of Jesus' passion. As her biographer Leo Madigan writes, "She would leave her bed and prostrate herself completely on the ground with her arms extended. At a certain point she would lift herself to a kneeling position, raise her eyes to heaven and open her hands in an attitude of offering her will to God. She repeated all of these gestures three times."[306] He continues, "Arriving at Calvary she would stretch herself out on the ground with her arms opened and her feet together, as if she were preparing to be crucified. . . . As the cross was lifted up, so Alexandrina lifted herself, as rigid as a corpse."[307] These actions, especially the bodily rigidity, would be difficult to explain in any case, much less in a case of medically-confirmed paralysis.

During one of her Friday ecstatic episodes, she had reached the stage of carrying the cross—the fourth Sorrowful Mystery. At that point, four men attempted to lift Alexandrina—but while she weighed less than eighty pounds, they were shocked that they failed to lift her. Madigan recounts, "When the ecstasy was over she was asked, 'Why is it that you weigh so much?' She answered, 'Because at that time I had the cross on my back.' Fr. Mariano asked her how much the cross weighed during these ecstasies. She answered in a simple but solemn voice, 'My cross has the weight of the world.'"[308] Madigan notes that Alexandrina endured these Friday stigmatic episodes on one hundred and eighty-two consecutive Fridays. Her ecstasies were well known by the people of Portugal, and by the end of her life, thousands of people were making pilgrimages to her house every day. Alexandrina da Costa was beatified in 2004 by Pope John Paul II.

At this point, it is easy to see a pattern emerging. Within the same year, just months after Our Lady of Fátima implored Catholics to do penance for poor sinners, Alexandrina da Costa, Marthe Robin, and Therese Neumann—three women who came from different countries and were strangers to each other—were each paralyzed [or suffered an injury that would leave her paralyzed]. Each went on to live a heroic life of sanctity. Each received the stigmata. It is also fascinating that each of these women had a devotion to Thérèse of Lisieux. Though Thérèse never exhibited the stigmata, she befriends those who receive this gift, as we will continue to see.

Servant of God Rhoda Wise (1888–1948) was born in a little town in Ohio about forty miles southeast of Canton. Rhoda's first husband passed away only a few months after their wedding, and Rhoda remarried—this time to an alcoholic, which led to much sadness, stress, and poverty for the family. She also developed a massive cyst and a terrible digestive disorder, which led to an abscess that required three medical operations. Thus, she spent considerable time at a local hospital run by the Sisters of Charity and known as the Mercy Hospital. Rhoda recounted, "During my long stay in the hospital, I, a Protestant, became interested in the rosary and had one of the sisters teach me how to say it. Soon after, I learned about Thérèse, the Little Flower of Jesus, and became greatly devoted to her, making one novena after another. I then felt myself drawn to the Catholic Church and after being instructed by Monsignor Habig, the pastor of St. Peter's Church, I was received by him on January 1, 1939."[309]

Though her spiritual life was blossoming, her health condition became much worse. She writes, "On February 12th, the doctor told me definitively there was no hope of a cure for my abdominal condition." With incurable cancer, there was nothing the doctors could do for her except discharge her on May 8 and let her die at home. Earthly physicians had been definitive about Rhoda's demise, but Christ—the Physician of Bodies and Souls—had a different plan. Twenty days after her discharge, Rhoda recounts that Jesus appeared to her in her room, "sitting on a chair beside my bed." She writes, "I said to him; 'Have you come for me?' His answer was, 'No. Your time has not yet come.'" On June 28th, Rhoda had another apparition of Jesus, accompanied by Thérèse. Rhoda recounts that Thérèse "placed her hand on my abdomen and said: 'I am the Little Flower. You have been tried in the fire and not found wanting. Faith cures all things.'" Her wounds were miraculously healed.

On Good Friday in 1942, Rhoda exhibited stigmatic wounds on her hands, feet, and head. She suffered from these wounds every first Friday from the hours of noon to 3 p.m.

until the year 1945. Many others witnessed these wounds, and thousands came to see her. Word began to spread that some people were healed through Rhoda's intercession, so many sick people came to see her. One of those people was named Rita Rizzo, a young woman who had suffered from terrible and dangerous stomach ailments of her own. At the time, Rita was not religious in any meaningful sense, but it was suggested that—in light of the rumors and reports—she try visiting Rhoda. The latter gave Rita a holy card of Thérèse that included a novena prayer, which Rita faithfully prayed.

At the conclusion of the novena, Rita was healed. Rita's biographer notes, "For Rita the healing was a transforming experience, a milestone that would entirely reorient her life."[310] That was no overstatement, for Rita Rizzo is better known by the religious name she later took: Mother Angelica. The foundress of EWTN—a network that has proclaimed, and continues to proclaim, the Good News around the clock and around the world—was miraculously healed after a visit to Rhoda Wise. Ten days before Rhoda died, Jesus appeared to her one final time with the message to exhort Catholics to pray the rosary for the conversion of Russia. She died on July 7, 1948—eleven wondrous years after the doctors had sent her home to die.

CONCLUSION

Now that we have studied most of the known blessed and canonized stigmatists from the time of Francis to the twentieth century, we must point out that the Church does not require our belief in these stigmatic events and episodes. Although a Catholic must assent to the dogma of the Immaculate Conception, for instance, no such assent of faith is necessary for the occurrences of mystical stigmata we have outlined in this book. For example, Catholics are free to believe that neither Padre Pio nor Faustina, nor Catherine of Siena ever had the stigmata at all. For that matter, Catholics are not required to believe in the Eucharist miracle of Lanciano, the appearance of Mary at Guadalupe, or the appearance of Jesus to St. Margaret Mary. In general, the Church has proven exceedingly cautious about miracles and the stigmata specifically.

With all this in mind, however, it is worth respectfully wondering if there has been an excess of ecclesiastical caution regarding miracles. Priests, bishops, and even popes make mistakes concerning miraculous events; as we have seen, Pope Pius XI admitted to one. Infallibility does not protect the pope from making imprudent judgments. Prelates have often urged caution about miracles, lest the faithful be deceived. To a point, that is understandable. But although certain prelates have exercised an abundance of caution, we might note that caution—properly speaking—is directed toward the good. As Aquinas phrased it, "Caution is required in moral acts, that we may be on our guard, not against acts of virtue, but against the hindrance of acts of virtue."[311] Caution should not be a hindrance to faith.

The stigmata are a mystical, yet physical, representation of the wounds of Christ in and on the bodies of those who love him. Moreover, this manifestation of wounds has borne tremendous fruits, both unseen and seen. In the realm of the unseen, the value of redemptive suffering will only be known in heaven. Regarding the visible, we must note that millions of people over the years (including the father of the author of this book) have been brought to the Catholic faith through the stigmata of others. Those conversions are verifiable.

Though faith does not require a Catholic to believe in the mystical stigmata, it is worth wondering if it is *reasonable* to refuse it. From a Catholic perspective, it seems odd to believe that even though the Catholic Church canonizes a woman who claimed to have the stigmata, her stigmata were a well-orchestrated hoax. This is why this book has focused primarily on those men and women who have been declared saint or blessed.

Prudence, defined by Aquinas as "right reason applied to action," dictates that we ask an important question: what is God doing with these miracles? What is he trying to show us? What does he want us to know? For instance, if the Mother of God did appear in Guadalupe and left a miraculous tilma (a position deeply held by this writer), it seems that she wants the world to know about it. Why the reluctance surrounding miracles? If miracles can lead others to the Church, why not tell others? As Jesus asked, "Is a lamp brought in to be put under a bushel, or under a bed, and not on a stand?" (Mark 4:21).

As we are about to see, there other miracles with a close connection to the stigmata that we should discuss and celebrate: they are eucharistic miracles.

5

FLESH AND BLOOD: THE INSEPARABLE CONNECTION BETWEEN THE STIGMATA AND THE EUCHARIST

> Let the entire man be seized with fear;
> let the whole world tremble;
> let heaven exult when Christ,
> the Son of the Living God,
> is on the altar in the hands of the priest.
>
> —St. Francis of Assisi[312]

A study of the lives of the blessed and canonized stigmatists illustrates some significant differences among them, but it also reveals some remarkable similarities; one of those similarities is an overwhelming devotion to the Eucharist. While this might not be surprising, what is more so is the frequency with stigmatists were favored with eucharistic miracles. Of course, eucharistic miracles have also been associated with non-stigmatist saints, but the percentage of these latter who experienced a eucharistic miracle is only a tiny fraction, whereas the percentage seems to hover around 100 percent in cases of saintly stigmatists. Why is it that miracles of the stigmata so often coincide with eucharistic miracles? As we will see, we are not talking about a few isolated eucharistic miracles; rather, many stigmatists exhibited ongoing miracles with Jesus in the Eucharist. Indeed, a comprehensive and detailed account of the eucharistic miracles experienced by the stigmatists could fill volumes, and this chapter offers only a tiny glimpse. We will also address one more miracle that was common among the women stigmatists: mystical espousal.

EUCHARIST & MASS, SACRIFICE & STIGMATA

To begin our discussion, we must take a closer look at the Eucharist. In his book *The Hidden Manna: A Theology of the Eucharist*, Fr. James O'Connor explains that "in the Eucharist, Christ is truly contained . . . the same body born of Mary, dead on the cross, raised gloriously from the tomb. It is not a different body from the one that 'sits at the right hand of the Father,' nor is it a part of that body, nor some kind of amorphous extension of that body. The Eucharist is the identically one, risen body of the Lord, only the mode or manner of presence differing from that which it exhibits in heaven."[313] The knowledge of this teaching is essential to make sense of the relationship between the stigmata and the Eucharist.

In short, by means of the Eucharist, Christ desires to include the entire Church in his sacrifice. Pope John Paul II explains this concept beautifully:

> The sacrifice of the cross is so decisive for the future of man that Christ did not carry it out and did not return to the Father until he had left us the means to take part in it as if we had been present. Christ's offering on the cross—which is the real Bread of Life broken—is the first value that must be communicated and shared. *The Mass and the cross are but one and the same sacrifice.* Nevertheless the eucharistic breaking of bread has an essential function, that of putting at our disposal the original offering of the cross. It makes it actual today for our generation. *By making the Body and Blood of Christ really present under the species of bread and wine, it makes—simultaneously—the sacrifice of the cross accessible to our generation,* this sacrifice which remains, in its uniqueness, the turning point of the history of salvation, the essential link between time and eternity[314] [emphasis added].

Today's Catholic faithful were not physically present at the foot of the cross, yet, mystically, we can still partake in that sacrifice as though we were. As John Paul II explains in his encyclical letter *Ecclesia de Eucharistia*: "By offering them his body and his blood as food, Christ mysteriously involved them in the sacrifice which would be completed later on Calvary" (21). Not only does the Eucharist allow the fruits of Christ's self-offering to be intimately communicated to each one of us, but "in giving his sacrifice to the Church, Christ has also made his own the spiritual sacrifice of the Church, which is called to offer herself in union with the sacrifice of Christ" (13).

Although Christ's sacrifice "was sufficient for the reconciliation of the entire world," explains O'Connor, nonetheless, "he willed and wills to associate us with that sacrifice."[315] We all share in Christ's royal priesthood at the cross and can make of our own lives and sufferings an offering with him to the Father in co-redemptive suffering. Far from being a morbid preoccupation with suffering, the Eucharist takes hold of a natural part of all human existence—suffering—and transforms it from consequence of sin to instrument of salvation. As O'Connor writes, Christ "willed to dignify and ennoble us, inserting into our own race the ability to satisfy for our evils."[316]

Although all the Catholic faithful participate to some degree in the satisfaction for sin obtained by Christ's redemptive self-offering, some men and women are able to participate in that satisfaction magnificently. And here, in this participation, we can begin to understand the stigmata. The stigmatist not only participates in this sacrifice, but provides a living reminder of Jesus' sacrifice on the cross. As we can see, there is an inescapable bond between the passion and death of Jesus, the Mass wherein this sacrifice is made present, and the Eucharist. Thus, it is fitting that those men and women who bear the wounds of Jesus' sacrifice also experience eucharistic miracles such as those described below.

EUCHARISTIC MIRACLES

Inedia. In outlining the various eucharistic miracles regarding the stigmatists, it seems appropriate to begin with this one: some stigmatists survived for many years on the Eucharist alone. That is to say, in some cases, their maximum daily intake of nourishment during multi-year periods was one single eucharistic host. St. Catherine of Siena lived for years solely on the Eucharist.[317] Bl. Anne Catherine Emmerich lived on the Eucharist alone for twelve years.[318] For fourteen years, Bl. Alexandrina da Costa lived exclusively on the Eucharist.[319] Like her, venerable Domenica Lazzeri survived for the final fourteen years of her life on the Eucharist alone.[320] Living on the Eucharist alone is called *inedia*.[321] Inedia is often mentioned in books about the stigmata, but it can be easily misunderstood, and some vital clarifications are necessary.

First, the miracle is not simply that these stigmatists *did not eat*. To intentionally deprive oneself of necessary nutrition is objectively disordered, but that is neither what these stigmatists intended nor accomplished. Instead—as Rene Biot explains—the miracle is that these stigmatists experienced "the suspension of all the needs of nutrition."[322] That is, they were miraculously fortified in the Eucharist alone. Various experiments confirmed that, although the stigmatists abstained from food, they did not lose weight. To add to that medically inexplicable fact, some stigmatists did not need water either. Medical research tells us that without any food, a person would die within weeks; without water, a person would die within days. Beyond the explanations of medicine, the Eucharist gave them the nutrients to survive, flourish, and exhibit remarkable energy.

Second, it was not that the stigmatists voluntarily refused to eat; rather, they could not digest earthly food. For instance, when Anne Catherine Emmerich was given food, she could not keep it down. Louise Lateau lived on nothing but the Eucharist for the last twelve years of her life, and detailed medical testimony confirms that she could not digest anything other than the Eucharist.[323] In fact, Lateau was able to receive the consecrated host every day yet was unable to digest an unconsecrated host.[324] The concept of inedia might sound quite sad, yet the stigmatists did not seem ever to have pangs of hunger or thirst. Their sole necessary nourishment was the Eucharist.

Communion from above. Another eucharistic miracle that the stigmatists experienced was the miraculous reception of the Eucharist from Jesus or an angel. We might simply term these miracles *Communion from above.* One of the most famous cases of this concerns Catherine of Siena. Bl. Raymond of Capua, Catherine's confessor and spiritual adviser, wrote a detailed and definitive biography of Catherine, in which he recounts that a particle of the consecrated host seemed to fall behind the altar when he said Mass one day after the consecration.[325] Frantically, he looked for that eucharistic particle, but he could not find It, which made him cry. Nevertheless, he finished Mass but afterward gave strict instructions that no one should go on the altar until he received advice about what to do next. He consulted a Carthusian priest named Dom Cristoforo and then went with him to see Catherine. When they finally located Catherine at another church, she was in an ecstasy. When she returned from her ecstasy, Bl. Raymond recounted the incident to Catherine.

"Did you look everywhere?" Catherine asked with a smile that seemed to indicate that she was already aware of what had happened.

Fr. Raymond assured her that he had looked everywhere, and Catherine responded again with a smile, "Why are you so upset about it then?"

At this point, Fr. Raymond began to sense that Catherine was involved, saying, "Mother, truly I believe it was you who took that bit of my host."

Catherine, never breaking her smile, responded, "Don't say it was my fault, Father! It was someone else, not me! Anyway, as far as that fragment is concerned, I warn you that you will never see it again."

Father then asked her in obedience to tell him what she knew about the missing host. Catherine replied, "Father, don't get upset about that fragment, for, to tell you the truth—as one must to one's confessor and spiritual father—it was brought to me, and when it was offered to me by Jesus Christ I took it." She said that Jesus "appeared to me and in his mercy offered me the fragment that he made you lose, and I received it from his most holy hands."

St. Angela of Foligno, whom we will learn more about in a moment, experienced both inedia and Communion from above. Imbert-Gourbeyre writes, "Angela was once communed by angels, and from that moment, she went twelve years without taking any food."[326] We find another example in St. Gemma Galgani. Due to illness, Gemma was sometimes unable to make it to Mass, and on some occasions, Jesus himself brought the Eucharist to her.[327] Her confessor notes that Gemma received the Eucharist at least three times directly from Jesus, and once alongside the Blessed Virgin Mary.[328]

St. Faustina details another such example in her *diary*. One night during her illness, Faustina was told that she was too exhausted to go to Communion the following day. Faustina was sorrowful at the thought of missing the Eucharist but accepted the sister's counsel. Faustina writes about what happened the next day: "In the morning, I made my meditation and prepared for Holy Communion, even though I was not to receive the Lord Jesus. When my love and desire had reached a high degree, I saw at my bedside a Seraph, who gave me Holy Communion, saying these words: 'Behold the Lord of Angels.'"[329] Faustina writes that the angel brought her Holy Communion for thirteen more days. She also provides a beautiful description of the angel: "The Seraph was surrounded by a great light, the divinity and love of God being reflected in him. He wore a golden robe and, over it, a transparent surplice and a transparent stole. The chalice was crystal, covered with a transparent veil. As soon as he gave me the Lord, he disappeared."[330]

Communion from a distance. Many of the blessed and saints also experienced what Biot calls "Communion from a distance."[331] These are cases in which the Eucharist miraculously traveled—as Alban Butler put it—"without visible agency," or more simply, without human hands to the tongue of the stigmatist.[332] Bl. Anna Maria Taigi provides an example. One day at Mass at the time of the Agnes Dei, the consecrated host suddenly left the hands of the priest and was suddenly in her mouth.[333] This was also witnessed to occur to Catherine of Siena multiple times.[334] Eyewitness testimony from Francesco Malevolti states, "I often saw her communicate . . . and I beheld how, when the priest was about to give her the Body of our Lord, before he had drawn more than a palm's length near her, the Sacred Host would depart out of his hands, and like an arrow, shoot into the mouth of the holy virgin."[335]

This was not a fanciful observation; Catherine's reception of Communion from a distance had been undoubtedly known to many others, including both priests and laity. In sworn testimony related to gathering evidence for Catherine's canonization, another priest named Bartholomew Dominic states that he witnessed it firsthand as he was approaching to give the Blessed Sacrament to Catherine.[336] He noted that he was initially concerned that the host would "fall to the ground; but It seemed to fly into her mouth."[337]

Eucharistic discernment. Some stigmatists were granted the ability of what we can term *eucharistic discernment.* That is, they could discern between an unconsecrated host and a consecrated one, despite there being no visible difference to the naked eye. We have already read about that in the case of Louise Lateau, but there have been others.

Venerable Ursula Benincasa (1547–1618) provides an excellent illustration of eucharistic discernment. Because her holiness was legendary, she was often put to various tests to determine her authenticity. On one such occasion, a priest tried to trick her by presenting an unconsecrated yet otherwise-identical-looking host. She quickly recognized this scandalous fraud of the priest and told him, "Believe not that I am permitted to fall into idolatry, and that I adore bread instead of the divine Redeemer."[338]

A similar event occurred in the life of Bl. Agnes of Jesus (1602–1634), a Dominican nun. Imbert-Gourbeyre tells us that one day her confessor, "curious to know if Mother Agnes was divinely enlightened as many claimed, presented her with an unconsecrated host instead of the Holy Eucharist. Agnes did not receive this bread but withdrew from the place where she was to commune. When questioned about her refusal, she told the confessor that he had only presented her with bread."[339]

Miraculous visions. Some stigmatists have been blessed with the ability to see God in the eucharistic host, including Angela of Foligno, whom Imbert-Gourbeyre numbers as a stigmatist. Born just twenty-two years after the death of Francis of Assisi, Angela was married with children, but her husband and children seem to have died at a very young age. As a widow, she became a Third Order Franciscan. Imbert-Gourbeyre writes that Angela asked "St. John and the Blessed Virgin to suffer the same pains they endured at the foot of the Cross, and her request was granted."[340] Thus, we could say that Angela suffered the vicarious pains of the Passion, which—from the perspective of the Blessed Virgin Mary—would be indescribably agonizing.

Regarding visions in the Eucharist, Angela stated, "Sometimes I see the host itself . . . and it shines with such splendor and beauty that it seems to me that it must come from God; it surpasses the splendor of the sun. This beauty which I see makes me conclude with the utmost certainty and without a shadow of a doubt that I am seeing God."[341] She describes another vision in which she saw Jesus: "I saw this with my bodily eyes. . . . When this vision occurred I did not kneel down like the others and I can't recall whether I ran right up to the altar or whether I was unable to move because I was in such a delightful contemplative state. . . . Christ was so beautiful and so magnificently adorned. He looked like a child of twelve. This vision was a source of such joy for me that I don't believe I will ever lose the joy of it."[342]

Faustina also experienced an event that can be placed into this category. In her diary, she recounts that Jesus told her of two religious sisters in danger of falling into mortal sin. Just after that discussion, Jesus said to Sr. Faustina, "I am going to leave this house . . . because there are things here which displease me."[343] After those words, the consecrated host flew from the tabernacle into her hands, so Faustina lovingly placed the Eucharist back in the tabernacle. The same thing happened a second time. Faustina writes, "Despite this, it happened a third time, but the host was transformed into the living Lord Jesus, who said to me, 'I will stay here no longer!' At this, a powerful love for Jesus rose up in my soul, I answered, 'And I, I will not let you leave this house, Jesus!' And again Jesus disappeared while the host remained in my hands. Once again I put it back in the chalice and closed it up in the tabernacle. And Jesus stayed with us."[344]

Another saint who had a vision of Jesus in the Eucharist was St. Catherine de'Ricci, who saw the Infant Jesus in the consecrated host. Moreover, Catherine saw that the expression of the Infant Jesus varied with each communicant. There was tremendous delight on the face of Jesus when some people received, and terrible unhappiness on his holy face when others received the Eucharist.[345] Another example is provided by Dominica of Paradise, who saw Jesus at the moment of the elevation of the Eucharist and received a drop of the Eucharist under the accident of wine on her tongue.[346]

MYSTICAL MARRIAGE

In addition to the miracle of the stigmata itself, ecstasies, and eucharistic miracles, there are many other wonders manifested in the stigmatists. Francis healed lepers. The Blessed Virgin Mary appeared and conversed with numerous stigmatists. Catherine of Siena had the power of exorcism; in fact, her power was so strong that her presence was enough for the devils to depart their victims and flee.[347] Catherine also levitated during ecstasies. Padre Pio could read hearts, a fact well-documented by numerous penitents over the decades. Lydwine could foresee the future. An encounter with Rhoda Wise healed Mother Angelica. As Antoine Imbert-Gourbeyre noted many years ago, it is clear that God delights in working miracles through those who bore his wounds.

But not all the marvels wrought by God in and through his stigmatists are of a miraculous nature. Others are mystical, emphasizing more the finality of the stigmata than their miraculous character. If some are granted a special share in the wounds of God, it is so that, by them, they might be brought into intimate union with him. The stigmata are, in a certain sense, a token pledged by the divine Bridegroom to his bride the Church, and it is fitting that they should culminate in what is called *mystical marriage*—or *spiritual marriage*.

To understand mystical marriage, we can begin by looking at the nuptial language of Sacred Scripture. In his classic text of mystical theology, Fr. Augustin Poulain points out that both testaments of Scripture repeatedly express the relationship between God and the Church in the language of marriage. In the Old Testament, we see the Lord constantly remonstrating with Israel, his wayward bride, calling her back to covenant fidelity. In the New Testament, sacramental marriage between husband and wife is designed to imitate the relationship of covenant fidelity between Christ and his Church: "Husbands, love your wives, as Christ loved the Church and gave himself up for her" (Eph. 5:25). Consecrated virginity, too, has a spousal connotation in Christianity and has frequently been referred to as "marriage with the divine Spouse."[348]

Both Poulain and Adolphe Tanquerey, author of *The Spiritual Life: A Treatise on Ascetical and Mystical Theology*, point to St. John of the Cross and St. Teresa of Ávila as the principal experts on spiritual marriage. Fr. Tanqueray writes that the "chief characteristics" of spiritual marriage are "*intimacy, serenity,*" and *"indissolubility."*[349] Intimacy produces serenity, which Tanquerey likens to the "peace and quiet rest as are enjoyed by married persons—who are sure of each other's love."[350] *Indissolubility* is the third characteristic of spiritual marriage, just as sacramental marriage is indissoluble. Teresa is careful to point out that a human in mystical marriage with God can still sin, but the soul in this state "refrains more carefully from committing the smallest offense against God."[351]

Indeed, what attraction could sin hold when one experiences the delights of an indissoluble spiritual marriage with God? We can conclude our description of the nature of spiritual marriage with Poulain's staggering definition: "It is a state in which the soul is habitually conscious of the divine co-operation in all her higher operations and in the depths of her being. No union of a more intimate kind can be imagined."[352]

Now that we have discussed some of the theology of mystical marriage, we can examine the ceremony of mystical marriage, perhaps best described in Bl. Raymond's biography of Catherine of Siena. By the time she turned nineteen, Catherine had already been living an exceedingly virtuous life, constantly praying and doing penance. Catherine also earnestly prayed that her faith be perfect and unshakable. While praying one day, she heard the voice of Jesus say, "I will espouse you to me in faith."[353] A few weeks before her twentieth birthday, Jesus appeared to Catherine and said, "Since for love of me you have forsaken vanities and despised the pleasure of the flesh and fastened all the delights of your heart on me, now, when the rest of the household are feasting and enjoying themselves, I have determined to celebrate the wedding feast of your soul and to espouse you in faith as I promised."[354]

As Jesus spoke, he was joined by the Blessed Virgin, St. Paul, St. John, and St. Dominic, along with King David playing the harp. The Blessed Virgin gently took Catherine's hand and led her to Jesus, where Jesus presented her with a gold ring inlaid with a diamond and four pearls. Jesus spoke to her the following words, "There! I marry you to me in faith, to me, your Creator and Savior. Keep this faith unspotted until you come to me in heaven and celebrate the marriage that has no end. From this time forward, daughter, act firmly and decisively in everything that in my Providence I shall ask you to do. Armed as you are with the strength of faith, you will overcome all your enemies and be happy."[355] Bl. Raymond explains that the diamond signified strength of faith, while the pearls signified purity of "intention," "thought," "word," and "deed."[356] Though no one else on earth ever saw the ring, Catherine saw it on her finger for the rest of her life. This event in Catherine's life was well known throughout much of Europe and was artistically re-created by some of the most famous Italian, Flemish, and Spanish artists in Christendom.

To be clear, thousands of saints have been canonized, but only a tiny fraction of saints have experienced mystical marriage; that said, it is fascinating that mystical marriage is almost common among canonized stigmatists. A partial list would include St. Mary Frances of the Five Wounds, St. Angela of Foligno, St. Colette, and St. Mary Magdalen de Pazzi, but many others. Fr. Poulain writes, "Our Lord gave rings to fifty-five persons, forty-three of whom had the stigmata."[357] Thus, there is a breathtaking link between the stigmata and mystical marriage.

CONCLUSION

When studying the biographies of the stigmatists, we must recognize that these men and women did not simply bear the wounds of Jesus; they were intimately close to Jesus. It seems their hearts beat in unison with the Sacred Heart of Jesus. For Catholics, their lives are inspirational and aspirational. Very few of us are called to be victim souls, but we are all called to follow Christ. And the stigmatists can show us the path to Christ.

Because these stigmatists provide such powerful examples and witnesses to us, it is sad that many of their stories are not well known. And in the case of saints, though their lives might be well known, their stigmata not always are. For instance, though many Catholics are familiar with St. Faustina, how many know she bore invisible stigmata?

At least in modern times, Catholics often seem reluctant to speak about miracles. Perhaps they embarrass us, or maybe we simply feel like we should not talk about those things that we cannot prove. But this gives rise to the question: what is proof? And how much evidence do we need before we can speak boldly about the stigmatic miracles or any miracles? That is something we will address in the following chapter. Now that we know the stories of the stigmatists, we need to know how to justify our belief in their miraculous biographies—both in our own hearts and minds and for the hearts and minds of those around us.

6

The Nature of Proof: An Analysis of Evidence, Burden, & Belief

> I feel that hoaxing—the proven explanation in numerous cases—provides the most credible overall solution to the mystery of stigmata. . . . It is well to consider whether St. Francis's own stigmata could have been faked.
>
> —Joe Nickell[358]

> The burden of proof is on the prosecution. The defendant doesn't even have to open his mouth.
>
> —Reginald Rose[359]

According to the skeptics, nearly everything you have just read in this book is wrong. Regarding the first chapter, the skeptics *might* concede that a person named Jesus once lived, but the Gospel accounts belong in the fiction category, and the whole notion of the Resurrection is laughably absurd. Regarding the second chapter, skeptics might concede that much of the account of St. Francis of Assisi is correct. Still, they would dismiss any supernatural element of the stigmata, perhaps explaining away the wounds of his hands and feet as a manifestation of leprosy. The third and fourth chapters—with their references to visions, ecstasies, repeated manifestations of the stigmata, and associated miracles—would strike skeptics as pure fantasy.

It is likely, however, the fifth chapter that would be treated as the most unbelievable, with the notion that bread and wine could become the body, blood, soul, and divinity of Jesus. The foundational and unwavering "belief" for a growing number of people is that there is no God. And if there is no God, it follows that there are no mystical stigmata—for there is no mystical *anything.* Thus, stigmatists—and all those who believe in the integrity of the stigmata—find themselves defendants in a mock trial that has already been decided.

It has been decided precisely because atheism is the prosecutors' starting point, just as atheism is their ending point. To borrow a term from economics, we might classify these folks as *efficient atheist* advocates. To explain that term, let's refer to the field of economics and the *efficient market hypothesis.* As CPA Rebecca Baldridge explains, "The efficient market hypothesis argues that current stock prices reflect all existing available information, making them fairly valued as they are presently."[360] In simpler terms, the theory posits that all relevant data is known and accurately priced by stock market participants, making it impossible to gain any advantage. However, this theory is widely and hotly disputed on Wall Street—even mocked.

The most famous ridicule of the efficient market hypothesis comes in the form of the following joke, which has been popular among economists for years. An efficient market theorist is walking down the street with a friend, and the friend announces, "Look, there is a twenty-dollar bill on the sidewalk!" The friend rushes to pick it up, but the economist yells, "You're wrong. That's not a twenty-dollar bill. It can't be. Because if it were, someone before you would have already pocketed it." We laugh at the expense—so to speak—of the efficient market theorist because he is so committed to his beliefs that he is insistent on rejecting something that can be seen and touched. However, this type of belief system is not unique to economics, nor is it always a laughing matter.

Along similar lines, there are also those whom we might classify as *efficient atheist theorists*. We might explain that term using a famous story told in metaphysics circles. One night, an astronomer (we'll call him "Mike") invited a fellow friend and astronomer (we'll call him "Andrew") to dinner one night. Mike was a Catholic, and Andrew was an atheist. When Andrew arrived at Mike's house, he marveled at a miniature planet model toy that Mike kept on his desk. When the toy was plugged into the wall, each planet moved in proper rotation around the sun. And each one was to scale: Jupiter was immense in proportion to Pluto. Andrew was delighted to watch this toy in action. And Andrew exclaimed in wonder, "Wow! Where did you get that?"

Mike replied, "I came home from work one day, and it was just here—right on my hobby table."

Andrew replied, "No, really! Where did you get it?"

Again, Mike replied, "I told you. It just showed up one day."

Andrew grew frustrated, "Look, if you don't want to tell me, that's fine. But don't make fun of me. Things like this don't just show up."

Mike replied, "No, they don't, do they? And this is only a toy. You believe that the actual universe just showed up—out of literal nothingness and nowhere."

Unaffected, Andrew stuck to his atheistic beliefs. (We might hope Andrew and Mike had a pleasant dinner anyway.)

In this story, Andrew is what we might call an *efficient atheist theorist.* Just as the efficient market theorist is willing to reject what can be seen and touched, so is the efficient atheist theorist. With a sweeping denial of both metaphysics and physics, the atheist's defining and unshakable belief is that there is no God. And if there is no God, there cannot be a miracle of the stigmata. The latter is the twenty-dollar bill. It is not there because it cannot be there—or so goes the theory. Armed with the belief that the experience of stigmata is false, the atheist calls us back, so to speak, assuring us there is nothing to see. There is little purpose in arguing against the ideology of inveterate atheism; like most logical fallacies, it presupposes what it wants to prove.

But one might argue that there is equally no evidence to suggest that the stigmata are "mystical," nor is there any evidence that the so-called "miracles" of the stigmatists are miracles. Refuting this position will be the focus of the remainder of this chapter and the foundational theme of the following two chapters. To do so, we will begin by discussing the nature of evidence and proof.

TESTIMONY, DOCUMENTS, AND TANGIBLE OBJECTS

Black's Law Dictionary defines *evidence* as "something (including testimony, documents, and tangible objects) that tends to prove or disprove the existence of an alleged fact."[361] Let's delve deeper into that famous legal dictionary and unpack this definition to see how it applies to the mystical stigmata.

Testimony is defined as "evidence that a competent witness under oath or affirmation gives at trial or in an affidavit or deposition."[362] Again, this needs a little unpacking because not all testimony is equal. For instance, *Black's* points out that the witness must be competent; ideally, he would be an expert. For example, if the case involves something of a medical nature, a licensed physician would be a highly competent witness. Of course, it would be even stronger if the physician were an eyewitness to the patient. That is gold-standard testimony. And even that testimony would be strengthened by the corroborating testimony of others, producing what *Black's* calls "cumulative testimony," that is, "identical or similar testimony by more than one witness."[363] *Black's* definition also points out that a sworn oath, while not necessarily in a formal jurisprudential setting, further galvanizes the weight of the testimony. Thus, we might say that the platinum-standard of testimony would be the sworn eyewitness affirmation of an expert corroborated by other eyewitness experts. As the preceding chapters testify, that is precisely the sort of testimony that has been offered to affirm the medical reality of the stigmata in certain well-documented cases.

Examples of such testimony about stigmatists abound, but we will reference just a few here. In chapter 4, for instance, we noted the extensive eyewitness medical documentation of Louise Lateau by doctors Molloy, Lefebvre, Imbert-Gourbeyre, and many others. As Michael Freze, author of *They Bore the Stigmata*, notes, Lateau "is one of the most thoroughly examined stigmatists of all time, having been subjected to countless tests and investigations by Church authorities, medical experts and psychologists."[364] That is no exaggeration. Entire commissions of doctors analyzed her case. Most famously, over three calendar years, a team of physicians with the Royal Academy of Medicine of Belgium analyzed Louise Lateau and concluded in agreement that her condition could not be explained by modern medicine.[365]

In chapter 3, we mentioned a postmortem examination of St. Veronica Giuliani, intended on corroborating or disproving the markings that Veronica had claimed were imprinted on her heart. That autopsy was performed by a surgeon named Dr. John Francis Gentili, who was accompanied by three other doctors named Bordiga, Falconi, and Giannini, a bishop, a governor, Veronica's confessor, an artist, two nuns, and several others.[366] After the autopsy, the following written statement of what they had seen was signed by those in attendance:

> Once the right ear [that is, atrium] of the heart was opened, the following were discovered: a beautiful cross, two flames, a spear, a rod, the seven wounds of Mary, a nail of the passion, a flag with the letters J and M (Jesus and Mary), a C in the cross (for charity), and above them the crown of thorns, and beneath the cross, the letters P and U (for suffering and humility; [Ita: *patire and umiltà*], so well-printed that a press could not have done a finer job.[367]

That constitutes testimony that is *eyewitness, expert*, and *corroborated*. Every court in the free world would classify this statement as robust evidence.

It is fascinating also that Veronica Giuliani was not the only person whose heart had stigmatic markings. By order of the pope, the body of St. Charles of Sezze was examined after his death, and it was discovered that the images of a crucifix and a roughly five-inch nail were on his heart—a fact documented by several doctors who were eyewitnesses.[368] Herbert Thurston also notes that Caterina Savelli, a reported stigmatic of the seventeenth century, had a deep injury in her heart that was discovered postmortem. Thurston writes, "The physician and the surgeon, who with many ecclesiastics signed the final attestation, declared that without supernatural intervention it would have been impossible for anyone to live with such a wound."[369]

The question might be naturally asked: how and why do we have such records? One of the reasons such powerful testimony exists is that when the Catholic Church is considering beatifying someone, witnesses are often called to make formal depositions under oath about the beatification candidate.

It would require many volumes to reference all the testimonies about all the stigmatists. In this section, we are simply establishing the point that, in sum, there has been a considerable body of gold-standard testimony in favor of stigmatists and their associated miracles for eight centuries.

Black's Law Dictionary defines *document* as "something tangible on which words, symbols, or marks are recorded."[370] *Black's* primary definition does not limit *document* to strictly legal documents such as written wills, ratified contracts, and notarized statements. Instead, *Black's* explains, "Most traditionally, of course, the term embraced any piece of paper with information on it." *Black's* secondary definition is similarly broad, encompassing "the deeds, agreements, title papers, letters, receipts, and other written instruments used to prove a fact." The critical point here is that a relevant document, even if it is not a strictly "legal document," can be considered evidence—potentially powerful evidence. Perhaps the most notable document among the stigmatists would be the *Praises of God* parchment written by Francis of Assisi, discussed in chapter 2. It falls into the category of evidence. The document category would also include biographies of the stigmatists, and a unique weight would be afforded to a biography penned by a witness who knew a person well. For instance, the writings of Thomas of Celano are a solid evidentiary document about Francis. Of course, it would also include autobiographies, such as that of Teresa of Ávila. Regarding the stigmatists, plenty of written material is available to peruse.

Tangible evidence is defined as "physical evidence that is either real or demonstrative."[371] Through the lens of the stigmata, the most obvious reference is to the first stigmata—the wounds of Christ—manifest on the Shroud of Turin. A person may certainly question whether the shroud is the actual burial cloth of Jesus, but it is an artifact that is difficult to explain otherwise. Tangible evidence also includes the incorrupt bodies of the stigmatic saints and the relic of the heart of Teresa of Ávila, which is still preserved.

In this conversation, one can reasonably assign various degrees of certainty or doubt as to the testimony, documents, and tangible evidence, but it is nevertheless evidence that should be submitted into the courtroom of one's own mind. A person might find various evidence inconclusive, but it is nonetheless evidence. To conclude that there is no evidence for the stigmata is either to misunderstand or to deny the very nature of what constitutes evidence. Someone could look at all the evidence presented in this book and dismiss it; indeed, some will. They could argue that looking at all this evidence does not "prove" anything. But that is not a fair assessment of what is meant by *proof.*

THE BURDEN OF PROOF

Various forms of evidence are used in the attempt to establish proof. But what, precisely, is *proof*? Does it mean absolute certainty? The American legal system recognizes two basic levels of burden of proof. In most *civil* cases, all that is necessary for a plaintiff/defendant to win is to prove his case to the judge or jury by a "preponderance of the evidence" which *Black's Law Dictionary* defines as "the greater weight of the evidence."[372] In percentage terms, it is anything more than 50 percent. Once a plaintiff makes it over the hurdle of 50 percent, he has legally "proven" his case.

A *criminal case,* however, demands more evidence: a judge or jury member must not find the accused "guilty" unless his guilt is believed to be *beyond a reasonable doubt.* And it is here—at this category of *reasonable doubt*—that things get truly fascinating. Preponderance of the evidence is easy to quantify in percentage terms, but where does "beyond reasonable doubt" occur in percentage terms? One might think it lies at 100 percent, when evidence meets the point of *elimination of any possibility to the contrary.* Yet, some of the highest-ranking judges in America do not agree with that standard; in fact, very few do. To illustrate this point, we can look to a study conducted in 1982 by the *Vanderbilt Law Review* that polled 171 "active, senior, and retired federal judges."[373] The study asked these prominent legal minds, "If you had to put a numeric value on 'beyond a reasonable doubt,' what would that percentage be?" Out of the 171 judges, the vast majority—150—provided a score lower than 100 percent. Over a hundred federal judges placed the percentage at 90 percent or less.

Let's now apply this to the stigmata. There are many centuries worth of gold-standard eyewitness testimony, first-hand written documents, and considerable tangible evidence in favor of the existence of the mystical stigmata. Using a standard burden of Western jurisprudence, "proof" has been achieved when we get past the 50 percent marker—preponderance of evidence. The question is: what is the evidence on the other side of the courtroom? And even if we were invoking the criminal standard of burden of proof, consider the following scenario.

If St. Padre Pio were on trial for the crime of bearing mystical stigmata, the prosecuting attorney would have a field day with a mountain of formidable evidence. What is the exculpatory evidence? What evidence exists that would acquit him? Had such a trial ever convened, Padre Pio would be looking at some serious jail time. To the stigmatist deniers and those who reflexively deny miracles broadly, it is fair to ask: what level of proof are you looking for? If one does not consider the mystical stigmata "proven" until it reaches 100 percent certainty, it must be said that this demands a higher level than is required at the most stringent level of American jurisprudence. And it is fair to ask as well: at what point is something ever proved true beyond all possible doubt? Doubt about the existence or explanation of a phenomenon always remains a moral possibility for those who prefer not to believe.

Astronomist Carl Sagan, who gained considerable fame in the 1970s and '80s from his PBS show *Cosmos*, posited that "extraordinary claims require extraordinary evidence." This quickly became a mantra of skeptics toward miracles. For example, if someone says that Teresa of Ávila had the mystical stigmata, an atheist might simply quote Sagan. However, there are two essential problems with this position. First, while it is true that the mystical stigmata are an "extraordinary claim," we do possess "extraordinary evidence" by any legal standard. Second, considering the voluminous gold-standard evidence involved, the "extraordinary claim" is not that incidents of mystical stigmata existed; rather, the "extraordinary claim" would be that there have not been any manifestations of the mystical stigmata. In other words, why is proving the stigmata the burden of the stigmatist? Why isn't disproving it the burden of the skeptic? It should be noted, that the simplistic and fanciful fallback claim that *God does not exist* is not evidence.

When we discuss any miracle, we might begin by honestly asking what level of proof we are searching for—and why. Regardless, it must be clearly stated that the function of apologetics, and of those who practice it, is not to definitively "prove" anything in this sense. We Catholics not only admit but profess openly that many things we believe are not *100 percent provable* in a scientific sense. After all, we practice the Catholic faith, not the Catholic proof. This is where the intersection of faith and reason meet. In these pages, we have put forward evidence and arguments that meet the beyond-reasonable-doubt standard of a supernatural phenomenon. For those initially disinclined to belief, this evidence may have served to a leap of faith, which alone can embrace the supernatural on its own terms. Very often, this happens in reverse order: first, we believe and then we use reason and the relevant sciences to explore and defend that belief. This *fides quaerens intellectum** approach to reality

* "Faith seeking understanding." This phrase enters Catholic theological tradition in St. Anselm's *Proslogion*, originally circulated, as he explains in the introduction, under the title *Fides Quaerens Intellectum*. In chapter 1 of the same, he explains: *Neque enim quaero intelligere ut credam, sed credo ut intelligam*. "I do not seek to understand in order that I may believe, but rather, I believe in order that I may understand." The complimentary roles of faith and reason in leading the human mind "into all the truth" (John 16:13) are amply explored in Pope John Paul II's encyclical letter *Fides et Ratio*.

is much of the reason that we have such a rich intellectual tradition in the Catholic Church. In the final analysis, everyone's mind forms a courtroom, and it is up to us to decide whether fair trials occur there.

CONCLUSION

One thing we have largely omitted in this chapter about evidence, proof, and trials is motive. In just about every trial, the question of motive arises. From the perspective of the Catholic faithful, the motive of the mystical stigmata has already been well established: the love and mercy of God, coupled with the willing participation of the stigmatist. But speculations about motive are quite different when it comes to those who do not believe in divine involvement. Because if one believes there is no divine intervention in the stigmata, he will often point to either fraud or insanity. To borrow the logic of C.S. Lewis, if the sacred is ruled out, we are dealing with either lying or lunacy. But if we can rule those out, we are left with only one possible explanation.

7

A QUESTION OF MOTIVE: WERE THE STIGMATISTS FRAUDSTERS?

A lie never lives to be old.

—Sophocles

Even if a skeptic ignores all evidence and proof about the stigmatists, he still has the burden of showing motive. Crimes have motives. If someone fakes the stigmata, it compels us to ask *why*. Leaving aside those persons who suffer from clinical pathological lying, people tell lies because they believe telling lies will benefit them in some way. Two of the strongest motivations include the desire for fortune and fame. We could even extend fame to include respect among one's peers, such as an order of religious sisters. Is it possible that some have faked the stigmata for these reasons? This chapter will investigate these motivations and the potential involvement of accomplices who would have been necessary to pull off the fraud. It will illustrate that neither fame nor fortune is a plausible explanation. This chapter will also explain in some medical detail why stigmata cannot be so easily faked.

FORTUNE & FAME

Some men and women have gained fame and fortune by appealing to religion—that is true. Even more specifically, some people have gained massive audiences and enormous wealth in the name of Christianity. Never has this been more obvious than in the rise of the "prosperity gospel." Bishop Robert Barron traces the movement back to Oral Roberts, while Kate Bowler, author of *Blessed: A History of the American Prosperity Gospel*, argues that the movement dates back to the late 1880s.[374] Bowler writes that the prosperity gospel "depicts faith as palpably demonstrated in wealth and . . . health. It can be measured in both the wallet (one's personal wealth) and in the body (one's personal health), making material reality the measure of the success of immaterial faith."[375]

Of course, the prosperity gospel's striking contradictions with Scripture are too numerous to catalog. Still, the critical point here is that evangelists of the prosperity gospel have become exceedingly wealthy through donations from listeners and viewers. A short list of prosperity gospel preachers has included Oral Roberts, Joel Osteen, Creflo Dollar, Kenneth Copeland, and many others. With some notable exceptions, most prosperity gospel leaders are not shy about their wealth; they openly flaunt it.

A 2006 article in *The New York Times* reported that Creflo Dollar owned multiple homes, jets, and Rolls-Royces.[376] Joel Osteen's mansion has an estimated value of about $15 million.[377] Kenneth Copeland tops them all. A 2021 story in the *Houston Chronicle* cited his net worth at over $750 million.[378] His primary residence in Fort Worth, Texas, is over 18,000 square feet. Copeland claims that God told him to build an opulent house for his wife, and of it he remarked, "You may think that house is too big. You may think it's too grand. I don't care what you think. I heard from heaven. Glory to God, hallelujah!"[379] Of course, this does not count his numerous vacation homes, which he flies to in private jets.[380] Just in case it does not go without saying, many of the prosperity preachers also have a philosophical aversion to poverty. Oral Roberts famously stated, "I tried poverty, and I didn't like it."[381] Kenneth Copeland has referred to poverty as a "curse."[382] He also said, "I hate poverty like God hates sin." It's difficult to imagine a stronger antithesis to Francis of Assisi's love of poverty than Kenneth Copeland's view of wealth.

Did the sainted stigmatists operate similarly? Were they searching for fame or fortune? As this book has illustrated, many stigmatists have freely chosen to live in cloistered convents and monasteries—that is, they decided to live almost entirely apart from the world. Choosing a secluded life would be very odd for someone deeply motivated by a desire for fame. As a 1984 article in the *British Medical Journal* observed, the stigmatists "did not seem to seek publicity or material reward—indeed, they often avoided it."[383] Fr. Thurston's book *The Physical Phenomena of Mysticism,* which provides significant biographical details about many of the stigmatists (as well as those whose stigmatic wounds he doubts), confirms the same. Thurston concludes, "Indeed, I might say in general that this intense unwillingness to court notoriety for any supernatural favor bestowed by God is the trait which has impressed me most deeply, and has seemed most uniform in the lives of those whom popular esteem, as well as the sentence of the Church, has proclaimed to be the truest followers of their Lord and heavenly Spouse."[384]

Even Louise Lateau desired anonymity; her story only rose to prominence because the prelates in her life bid her make herself available for medical study. There is no doubt that Louise came to fame; Belgian newspapers mentioned her in dozens of news stories between 1873 and 1883. But Louise, like other stigmatists, never asked for fame nor wanted fame. From the perspective of the Catholic faith, it's easy to see why: they wanted to practice humility. It's also easy to see why on a temporal level. Many stigmatists were held in derision. In some cases, even their fellow Catholics and members of their own religious orders were embarrassed by them. Many Catholics eschew reference to miracles of any sort lest they be mocked for such beliefs. Even Catholic Church officials have often treated those with the stigmata wounds harshly. Nevertheless, their treatment by anti-Catholics, desperate to advance the narrative that stigmatists are frauds, has been far worse.

An article in the *Journal of Religious History* recounts an incident that gives us a fair estimation of the level of hatred directed against stigmatist Louise Lateau:

> On 7 March 1875, a carnival procession made its way through the streets of Brussels. On one of its wagons, a devil aimed his trident at a life-size doll of a peasant woman in a grey dress with a white bonnet, her hands and feet covered in red paint. She was hanging from a scaffold and had a cauldron at her feet. For anyone who wondered about the identity of the unlucky girl, a sign on the doll spelled the name: 'Louise La Peau,' a play on the name of the famous Belgian stigmatic, Louise Lateau (1850–1883)."[385]

It is little wonder that stigmatists attempted to avoid fame. Did the stigmatists desire material fortune? To analyze that question, we can begin by looking at Francis of Assisi, who received the stigmata just two years before his death. Lest we forget, Francis grew up in an inordinately wealthy household as the son of a successful businessman. However, Francis gave it all up—opting instead for absolute poverty. It is not disputed by any credentialed biographer, Catholic or otherwise, that Francis lived in abject poverty as part of his calling. Is anyone seriously positing that Francis, who renounced his family fortune and gave away all he had to the poor, chose near the end of his life to fake the first stigmata in a desperate effort to regain his wealth? The very idea of leveling the charge of material greed against Francis is, quite literally, laughable. Nearly all the blessed and canonized stigmatists lived in poverty; indeed, many of them took a formal vow of poverty in a religious order. But beyond the poverty of the blessed and saints of several centuries ago, poverty was also the condition of modern stigmatists such as Louise Lateau and Rhoda Wise.

Other than a few months of her life in which she lived as a servant, Lateau lived in the same tiny family cottage from the time of her birth to the time of her death thirty-three years later.[386] In his 1869 biography of Lateau, Lefebvre described the family cottage in detail. Besides a storage space above and a tiny cellar below, the house had one living space consisting of two rooms on a dirt floor. One room was used "as a kitchen and general living room" that was about two hundred square feet; the second room was about half the size and served as a bedroom for everyone.[387] Lefebvre writes that the family's house was "truly of the poorest."[388] At the height of her fame, Lateau's possessions seemed to consist of a bed, some bedding, a small table with fake flowers, a few articles of clothing, a small linen cloth, a few crucifixes and religious pictures, and a blood-stained wooden chair.[389]

Louise Lateau's case went beyond garden-variety poverty. It was widely believed that Lateau did not eat any food for at least seven years of her life. Instead, she existed solely on the Eucharist. Even non-Catholics were aware of this widespread claim. In the anti-Catholic hysteria of the time, there was a cartoon distributed that caricatured Lateau hiding a large turkey under her bed. The implication was that Lateau feasted sumptuously when no one was looking—which was almost never, considering her vast number of visitors. Whether a skeptic today believes that Lateau could survive on the Eucharist alone, it is clear that if gaining fortune—or even the gift of a cold sandwich—were Lateau's master plan, she failed miserably.

Therese Neumann was born poor and remained poor. A March 27, 1948 article in *The New York Times* reported that five thousand people had gathered at her home the day before to see her stigmata. That article described her house as a "simple yellow stucco cottage."

Rhoda Wise's conditions were no better. Rhoda lived in a tiny one-story house by the town dump in Canton, Ohio, when she received the stigmata. Hundreds, even thousands of people, visited her some days, but she never relocated. After receiving the stigmata, she continued living in that same house until her death. As of June 2023, Redfin estimated the *current* value of the house and property to be a mere $60,586. (For a comparative reference, the median price of a home sold in America in 2023 is well over $400,000.)

Which of the canonized or beatified stigmatists became highly paid public speakers? Which of them had a mansion? Which of them died with gold hidden behind her walls or money stashed under her bed? Which of them lived in luxury? The truth is that all the canonized and beatified stigmatists lived the virtue and the reality of poverty.

THE PAINFUL PRICE OF CELEBRITY

Even if someone believes that fame and fortune are the driving forces behind fraudulent stigmata, there remains the unexplained dilemma of self-inflicted injuries; simply put, if the stigmatists are lying, they would have to be regularly inflicting deep wounds upon themselves. That would constitute a hefty price to pay. This fact is dismissed far too casually by skeptics. For example, the *Wikipedia* entry for St. Gemma Galgani (1878-1903) offers these explanations to refute her claims of having the wounds of stigmata:

> The physician Pietro Pfanner, who had known Galgani since her childhood, examined her stigmata. . . . and noted spots of blood on the palms of her hands but when he ordered the blood to be wiped away with a wet towel there was no wound. He concluded the phenomenon to be self-inflicted. On another occasion Galgani's foster mother Cecilia Giannini observed a sewing needle on the floor next to her. The psychologist Donovan Rawcliffe claimed in a book published nearly fifty years after her death that her stigmata were caused by "self-inflicted wounds of a major hysteric."[390]

This entry constitutes a typical but unserious dismissal. A mountain of forensic evidence has been produced for numerous stigmatists by the highest-credentialed physicians in Europe, and the skeptics are entirely inveterate. It suffices that a sewing needle lies on the floor of Gemma Galgani—a seamstress by profession—to be considered unshakable evidence of her fraud. And if blood appears where no visible wound is found, this is somehow considered to be evidence that the invisible wound is self-inflicted! This opinion, put forward by Rawcliffe, reads in full, "Gemma Galvani's [sic], painful stigmata were, beyond the slightest shadow of doubt, the self-inflicted wounds of a major hysteric."[391] To corroborate the use of a term like "beyond the slightest shadow of doubt," one would expect such a claim to be followed by various citations of firsthand witnesses and medical documents from high-credential physicians. But Rawcliffe offers exactly none: no footnotes, no references, no citations, no explanatory notes, no testimony, no documents. Nothing.

As the Wikipedia entry illustrates, sooner or later, regardless of evidence, almost all the skeptics offer self-infliction as a dismissive explanation. To those unacquainted with the stigmata, this might sound reasonable at first. After all, some soldiers have shot themselves in an attempt to make it look like enemy fire to get out of combat. Couldn't the stigmatist do just the same thing? The short answer is that the nature of stigmatic wounds is unique—unlike any other wounds. Self-infliction is not easy to explain for three main reasons: *first*, the highly bloody nature of the stigmata; *second*, the transitory duration of stigmatic events; *third*, the likelihood of infection—and the unlikelihood of surviving infection.

Bloody nature. As this book has illustrated, the wounds of the stigmatists were witnessed to be extremely bloody. For instance, witnesses noted that Francis of Assisi's cassock was often soaked in blood. One of the doctors observing Louise Lateau pointed out that it was difficult for him to get a dermatological sample from her scalp because her hair was soaked with blood. Padre Pio lost eight ounces of blood every day from the wound in his side alone—not to mention blood lost from the wounds in his hands and feet.[392] Although Francis and Francesca lived before photography, recent cases of blood-drenched stigmatists are photographed. Pictures were taken of the stigmatist Rhoda Wise that show blood that had gushed from her head wound into her eyes and onto her face. Pictures illustrate that Therese Neumann's wounds were similarly bloody. The pictures are difficult to look at without cringing. As we have seen, many hundreds of doctors have confirmed this blood flow. Could these, and so many other stigmatists, simply be committing self-injury?

And before answering that question, we must consider that it is not just *external* bleeding but *internal* injury that must be accounted for. Teresa of Ávila and Therese Neumann had medically verified heart wounds. An autopsy was performed on stigmatist Veronica Giuliani, during which two physicians and other witnesses saw the unmistakable imprint of a cross upon her heart. How does a person not only give herself a heart laceration but survive for years afterward?

Transitory wounds. As the previous chapters have referenced, a stigmatist might endure her wounds for years or even several decades, but the acute bleeding of the wounds typically happened on a tight weekly schedule. In many cases, the bleeding regularly began on Thursday nights and subsided on Fridays or Saturdays. For instance, Louise Lateau's Friday stigmatic wounds generally healed within a few days. Considering the severity of the wounds, that would be almost impossible to explain even once. But Lateau experienced this same process nearly every week—week after week—for fifteen years until her death. Doctors sometimes use the term "fast-healer" to describe certain patients, but quickly healing from stigmatic wounds has no medical explanation. After all, these are not paper cuts and pinpricks; instead, they are skull-deep head wounds that cause profuse hemorrhages, shoulder gashes, side wounds that travel deep into the thorax, and hands and feet wounds that nearly form holes. How can this sort of wound heal within a few days? The *self-infliction* of wounds is certainly possible, but the weekly *self-healing* of open wounds has no medical explanation.

Lack of infection. It is easy to forget in our modern medical age, but nearly every stigmatist discussed in the book exhibited stigmatic wounds before the pivotal discovery of antibiotics. If Louise Lateau had inflicted bloody injury on herself eight hundred times, the physical trauma would have been death-defying in many ways, but perhaps none so astonishing as the lack of infection. To understand why this is so medically baffling, consider the words of David Gratzer, author of *The Cure: How Capitalism Can Save American Health Care*. Gratzer writes,

> It's easy to forget how different the world was before penicillin. Rich and poor could die of infection within one or two days. As president, Calvin Coolidge had access to the best doctors in the country, but it did little good when his son fell ill in 1924. At age sixteen, Calvin, Jr. enjoyed tennis on the White House courts. Playing one day without socks, he developed a small blister, which became infected. He died soon after. . . . "In his suffering, he was asking me to make him well," remembered Coolidge. "I could not."[393]

Until the early 1940s, people routinely died from infection. As Eric Lax notes in *The Mold in Dr. Florey's Coat*, a scratch or even "the smallest cut could lead to a fatal infection." Indeed, it often did. Happily, in the most extraordinary stroke of medical serendipity in history, Alexander Fleming discovered penicillin and tens of millions of lives were quickly saved. Gratzer notes that "penicillin has spared countless other parents from such heartbreaking helplessness." The work of medical researchers such as Fleming, Healy, Chain, and Florey led to the mass production of penicillin and changed the world. But before penicillin, something as minor as a blister could spell death within forty-eight hours.

So we are to believe that Lateau (to name just one example among stigmatists who lived before the advent of antibiotics) inflicted hundreds of bloody assaults upon her head, hands, shoulder, and feet on eight hundred separate weekly occasions—yet never developed an infection? No one should have been able to survive Lateau's abundant hemorrhages in any age, much less an age absent antibiotics. Yet Lateau lived with the stigmata for fifteen years. If that was the case, skeptics should be celebrating a different miracle—a miracle of no infection.

PARTNERS IN CRIME?

If the stigmata were hoaxes, those women and men pretending to be stigmatists would have needed plenty of accomplices, including an inner sanctum network of licensed physicians, nurses, priests, bishops, and other eyewitnesses. Moreover, these people would have been so adamant about maintaining the fraud that they were willing to take the secret to their deaths without ever breathing a word about it. Is all this possible? Is this reasonable to believe?

Let's begin by looking at the possibility of a Catholic Church conspiracy.

Non-Catholics might be under the impression that the offices of the Catholic Church are eager to approve and promote miracles, but that is almost never the case. Throughout the ages, Catholic Church officials have proven quite cautious—sometimes in the minds of the laity, almost *aggravatingly* cautious—about miracles. Except in rare cases, the Church merely "approves" a miracle for optional belief. And even when the Church approves a miracle, this does not typically mandate belief in that miracle. Belief in miracles—

except for those involving dogmas such as Christological and Marian dogmas, for instance—is not required. For example, a Catholic is required to believe that Jesus rose from the dead; he must also affirm that Mary was assumed body and soul into heaven.

However, a Catholic is not required to believe that St. Bernadette is incorrupt or that the Shroud of Turin is the authentic burial cloth of Jesus. He may refuse belief in the miracle of Lanciano, the tilma of Guadalupe, the double-helix "St. Joseph staircase" in New Mexico, the appearance of Mary at Fátima, and the stigmata of Padre Pio. The Church does not require an assent of faith to any of these. *The New York Times* reported the sun's miracle in Fátima, but a Catholic is not required to believe in that miracle at all. Further, the Catholic Church does not require a belief in anyone's stigmata (outside the wounds of Jesus himself). At a certain point, it would be incongruous for a Catholic to reject all these miracles, but the fact remains: he is not required by the Catholic Church to believe them.

Church officials were not only reticent to promote miracles, but they also clamped down on the belief in some miracles. When the faithful began to publicize that he bore the stigmata, Padre Pio was disallowed from saying public Masses. Further, he was not allowed to exhibit his wounds. His suppression occurred by papal decree, and it took years to even partially reverse the decision. Or, to give another example, the Holy See officially banned the *Diary of Saint Faustina* from 1959 to 1979.[394]

Even if the official acts involving Padre Pio and St. Faustina (at least partially based on misinformation) were eventually overturned, clearly we are still a long way from unscrupulous prelates going rogue to make money and generate fame. Indeed, there have been such prelates in history;

history records the scandalous actions of those who used their ecclesiastical positions to advance their status, power, and wealth. How did such self-serving ecclesiastics treat miracles and those directly involved with them? Providing a short yet comprehensive answer to that question is impossible: there are simply too many miracles and self-serving prelates to reference. However, we can cite some of the most well-known cases, beginning with the treatment of St. Joan of Arc.

Joan of Arc seemed surrounded by miracles from her adolescence until her death. According to her testimony, she conversed with three saints in heaven and learned from a heavenly voice where to find a mysterious sword she would carry into battle; no less miraculous was the saving of her nation on the battlefield. The reaction of prelates toward Joan—prelates of her nation, no less—was grievous, calculated, and murderous. Rather than celebrate her miracles, she was absurdly charged with both witchcraft and heresy. Joan was tried in Rouen, France, by Catholic officials who subjected her to malicious injustice and torture.

In his book *Heroes*, historian Paul Johnson notes that Joan was allowed neither a defense lawyer nor witnesses in her trial.[395] In the end, she was burned to death, and her ashes were dumped into the River Seine. Johnson writes, "The French have always in modern times blamed the English for what happened to Joan. . . . But the crime, if it was a crime, was a French one."[396] But more to the point, this was not a crime of state but of church officials. As Johnson points out, "The two judges were Pierre Cauchon, bishop of Beauvais, in whose diocese her supposed offenses had taken place, and the deputy inquisitor of France, Jean Lemaistre, Dominican prior of Rouen."[397] He continues, "We have a complete list of those who took part in the trial: one cardinal, six bishops, thirty-two doctors of theology, sixteen bachelors of theology, seven doctors of medicine, and 103 others. Of these only eight were English, of whom two attended regularly but took no part in the process. . . . Her chief enemy was not really the English but the Church."[398]

Though Joan of Arc's case was extreme, it illustrates a principle. Most miracles are attached, in a sense, to a person. For example, the healing spring at Lourdes was first revealed to St. Bernadette; the tilma of Guadalupe was the personal garment of St. Juan Diego; the miracle of the sun at Fátima will be forever associated with the three children seers. If a prelate were to promote these miracles, it might serve to glorify Joan, Bernadette, and Juan, but it would do little to glorify himself. In fact, it would potentially distract from his prominence. To illustrate this point, consider the following. Even in our day, millions of sick and infirmed people make pilgrimages to Lourdes every year. We could guess that most of them are familiar with Bernadette and her biography in some detail. But how many of those same pilgrims could name the current bishop of Lourdes, or for that matter, any bishop in the entire history of Lourdes? I would guess the number is close to zero. As the case of Joan illustrates, self-serving prelates tend to squash those associated with miracles—not promote them. If there is a way for self-serving prelates to parlay miracles into personal wealth, they don't seem to have found it.

Of course, even if the Catholic Church did manage a way to form such a silent and widespread conspiracy, there remains the problem of the doctors—because they would need to be part of the conspiracy also. Not every stigmatist in history has received acute medical and scientific testing; however, many stigmatists *have* received such extensive medical observation. Even hundreds of years ago (as we have detailed in previous chapters), autopsies have confirmed medically inexplicable stigmatic wounds. Some modern stigmatists like Lateau, Neumann, and Padre Pio were carefully observed by medical personnel for much of their lives. A 2018 article in the *Journal of Religious History* notes, "A riddle to modern science," Lateau "was studied by no fewer than one hundred doctors."[399] In reality, the actual number is easily triple that estimate. Each of these doctors conducted his own observations and tests; thus, thousands of tests were performed. It is unfeasible to cite them all, but an experiment conducted on Lateau in 1875 provides an excellent example.

Aware of the notion that Lateau's bleeding systematically began on Thursdays, a medical team led by Dr. Warlomont encased her entire right hand and arm into a glass tube with a seal that could not be broken without evidence of its breakage. This left Lateau with no opportunity for her (or anyone else, for that matter) to inflict wounds upon herself. The next day, Friday, Warlomont and his associate Dr. Crocq noted that the glass tube had not been broken or tampered with. They also noticed something else: five grams of fresh blood in the tube and freshly coagulated blood on her wounds. Warlomont firmly concluded, "It seems to me, therefore, that the hemorrhages appeared spontaneously and without the intervention of external violence."[400] The following year, after even more tests, the doctors of the Belgian Academy concluded their two-year investigation by declaring—in a signed statement—that science and medicine could not explain Lateau's stigmata. Even skeptic Donovan Rawcliffe admits in *Occult and Supernatural Phenomena* that "the stigmata of Louise Lateau were subjected to strict medical observation by the Belgian Academy of Medicine."[401]

Some adamantly skeptical physicians refused to accept those findings; they mocked the two-year study's findings without ever conducting a study of their own. Maybe they were afraid of what they might see. One of these physicians was Rudolf Virchow, who is known as the "father of modern pathology." Virchow had seen medical reports about Lateau but insisted they must be fraudulent. If the reports were true, Virchow insisted, then "all the laws of nature are contradicted in Louise Lateau."[402] That's an ironic statement, for what Virchow was really saying—albeit accidentally—was this: if the findings of the Belgian Academy are accurate, we must discuss the possibility of divine intervention and whether these wounds indeed constitute mystical stigmata. Nevertheless, he would not visit her. This is standard practice for the skeptics over the years. Perhaps they thought that seeing might lead to believing, which was deemed unthinkable.

It's important to make one last point about Virchow—one that has far-reaching implications about much of what is discussed in this book. In a previous chapter, we discussed the case of Ignaz Semmelweis and how his colleagues treated him miserably and dismissed his extensive research on puerperal fever. One of the chief physicians that rejected Semmelweis and his verifiable findings was none other than Rudolf Virchow. At first merely dismissing the findings, Virchow spent several years openly attacking Semmelweis and his research both in writing and professional lectures.[403] Considering his widespread influence, Virchow's "disdainful silence" and then outspoken rejection of Semmelweis's ultimately led to the deaths of countless women.[404] As a biographer of Semmelweis writes, the "incessant attacks" by Virchow "upon the man who had devoted his entire existence to the study of puerperal fever continued to exert their deleterious effects upon Semmelweis's psyche."[405] As the previous chapter referenced, these attacks eventually drove Semmelweis into an asylum.

What made it so hard for Virchow to accept the findings of Semmelweis? For that matter, what made it so hard for him to accept the findings of the doctors who had extensively studied Lateau? We could write it off simply as overwhelming hubris, but that would be too simplistic, because Virchow's actions and writings illustrate something more. Virchow provided a textbook illustration of what has come to be known as the *Semmelweis Reflex*, which is defined as "a human behavioral tendency to stick to preexisting beliefs and to reject fresh ideas that contradict them (despite adequate evidence)."[406] In fairness to Virchow, he was not the only one who exhibited this tendency; rather, it has been a common response to the stigmatists for centuries.

Happily, there were many physicians who did not succumb to the Semmelweis Reflex. Often, those who actually observed the stigmatists (including, as we have seen, anti-Catholics) were the *most* convinced of the authenticity of their stigmata. A December 1984 article in the *British Medical Journal* makes the ironic observation that "Therese Neumann was observed constantly on several occasions, but this satisfied only the observers, not the critics."[407]

Of course, this leads us back to the fundamental question of motivation. What could have motivated hundreds of doctors to contrive such a stigmatic plot? Some of those who affirmed the stigmata were held in derision and removed from their posts; thus, the motivation of fame seems extremely unlikely. As for fortune, neither stigmatist nor stigmatist apologist ever seemed to have money.

In sum, it simply does not seem credible that a vast conspiracy of churchmen and physicians could have quietly carried on the hoax of the stigmata.

CONCLUSION

For a skeptic to posit that stigmatists are liars is to indict hundreds of people, from Francis of Assisi to Catherine of Siena to Padre Pio. But as we've discussed here, it is not simply to accuse them of fraud but to credit them with pulling off some of the most incredible and death-defying physical feats imaginable. Their con would be even more impressive considering that it would require tricking some of the best and brightest medical minds in Europe and America. Is it possible that they simply hoodwinked the doctors and nurses? Is it possible that these conspiracies between prelates and physicians just keep occurring? After all, widespread lies require widespread accomplices.

Ironically, the big money has not been made in the affirmation of a miracle, but in its denial. If a Catholic writes a book about Fátima, it might sell a few thousand copies. If one writes a book denying the miracle of Fátima, it can become a bestseller. Which of the so-called "Four Horsemen of Atheism"—Christopher Hitchens, Richard Dawkins, Sam Harris, and Daniel Dennett—is not wealthy?

The skeptic can gleefully point to the fact that some people in history have faked stigmata. In response, we concede the point: not everyone who claimed to have the stigmata really did. Herbert Thurston writes, "That some instances of alleged stigmatization are simply fraudulent is not to be disputed. The two notorious religious impostors of the sixteenth century, Magdalena de la Cruz and Maria de la Visitacion, both professed to bear the marks of the passion in hands, feet, and side."[408] Of course, their fakery was discovered. As this book has illustrated, stigmata are difficult to fake. But beyond that, the fact that one or another person has faked the stigmata has zero bearing on Catherine of Siena, Teresa of Ávila, Padre Pio, and many others. Imagine that

John Smith claims the ability to run a four-minute mile. He brags about it all the time. After a while, his friends call his bluff. They take him to a local track and time him with a stopwatch. John Smith doesn't even come close. He clocks in at twelve minutes. But does John Smith's fraudulent claim mean that *everyone* who makes that same four-minute claim is lying? Clearly not. To prove that the four-minute mile can be run, all one must do is show that one person ran a four-minute mile. Similarly, it is not the burden of a Catholic apologist to prove that *every* claim of stigmata is real. To substantiate that miraculous stigmata are a genuine mystical occurrence, the Catholic apologist only needs to illustrate one single case. Just one. From there, we can attempt to determine how many cases are credible.

This leaves us with one final skeptical objection: that the stigmatists might have been *crazy*, somehow producing the wounds with their minds. We will address that question in the coming chapter.

8

BY REASON OF INSANITY: WERE THE STIGMATISTS LUNATICS?

Most scientists and other scholars are unfamiliar with the intellectual scaffolding that reveals the compatibility between all scientific findings and a conception of God as radically transcendent creator of all that exists.

—Brad S. Gregory[409]

No power of auto-suggestion, no abnormal pathological conditions, could enable a contemplative to evolve from the flesh of his hands and feet four horny excrescences in the form of nails, piercing his extremities and clinched at the back. Such a manifestation, if it occurs, must surely be held miraculous.

—Herbert Thurston[410]

In the preface to his 1894 book, *La stigmatisation*, Antoine Imbert-Gourbeyre illustrates that modern scientists often begin analyzing stigmatization by snubbing or denying the very existence of the supernatural. A case in point is Professor Charcot, whom Imbert-Gourbeyre praises as a man who made significant advances in studying nervous disorders. But Charcot made the foundational and critical mistake of simply diagnosing stigmatism as a nervous disorder or hypnotic trance:

> In all these matters of higher order, Charcot, his students, and followers only revealed their ignorance and ineffectiveness; some even displayed dishonesty. Master and disciples ventured into unfamiliar territory, ignoring or perhaps unaware that there existed an established experimental science for supernatural phenomena: mystical theology. They should have consulted and questioned the original observers about the facts they presented; it would have been only fair.[411]

Worse, Charcot did not limit his comments to those stigmatists in his day, such as Louise Lateau; instead, Charcot went back in history to accuse sainted stigmatists of mental disorders. The list even included St. Francis of Assisi and St. Teresa of Ávila, the latter deemed an "undeniable hysteric."[412]

Beyond the casual dismissal of stigmatists, Charcot seemed to paint all supernatural events—specifically those relative to the Catholic faith—with the same brush.

> More gravely, Charcot, a free thinker of the worldly kind, made the mistake of going outside of his role and competence. He attempted to use hysteria and hypnotism

> to challenge supernatural phenomena such as stigmatization, divine ecstasy, the miracles of Lourdes, and demonic possessions. From the perspective of science, he should have confined himself to the study of observable and quantifiable phenomena, but he went far beyond that.[413]

Of course, Charcot was not alone. In the past two centuries, many professional psychologists and others have posited mental illness as a possibility—or probability—for the stigmata. What they have consistently failed to do is illustrate how mental illness can produce the wounds of the stigmata, or for that matter, anything like them. This chapter will debunk the lunacy position.

AN "ENLIGHTENED" POSITION

Since the Enlightenment, accusations of lunacy against stigmatists have become commonplace. Of course, the charge has not been reserved for stigmatists—far from it. Accusations of insanity have been employed as the opening salvo in the entire discussion of Christian belief. In other words, lunacy is not just a charge against stigmatists specifically but a general charge against all those who believe in the divinity of Christ. To "enlightened" minds, the *stigmatist*, the *woman who believes in the Eucharist*, and the *man who believes that God created the universe* are all crazy. Many of the enlightened have not only an anti-Catholic perspective but also a violently hateful one. From the perspective of Catholic apologetics, it is important to recognize the intellectual bias of our interlocuters, lest we spend too much time and energy trying to defend the sanity of intellectual giants such as St. Catherine of Siena and St. Teresa of Ávila.

The *Enlightenment* is the name given to a movement beginning in the seventeenth century that jettisoned the Catholic religion in favor of an alternative world-view. There is no official list of its proponents, but major contributors to Enlightenment philosophy include Jean-Jacques Rousseau, Voltaire, Baruch Spinoza, Edward Gibbon, Immanuel Kant, Denis Diderot, George Berkeley, and David Hume. The Enlightenment is often linked with what is called the Scientific Revolution; proponents of the Enlightenment generally advance the idea that the Catholic Church kept man in darkness, while this new movement finally "enlightened" man's reason and creativity.[414] Of course, the idea that the Catholic Church was anti-science or that the Church stifled man's creativity is nonsense. Rodney Stark, author of *Bearing False Witness: Debunking Centuries of Anti-Catholic History*, provides a factual and powerful defense of the Catholic Church against Enlightenment theorists. To start with, the entire notion of the "Scientific Revolution" was fictional. Stark writes, "the notion of a Scientific Revolution was invented to discredit the medieval Church by claiming that science burst forth in full bloom only when a weakened Christianity no longer could suppress it."[415]

Stark points out, however, that "the great scientific achievements of the sixteenth and seventeenth centuries were produced by a group of scholars notable for their piety, who were based in Christian universities, and whose brilliant achievements were carefully built upon an invaluable legacy of centuries of brilliant Scholastic scholarship."[416] In essence, what is referred to as the "Scientific Revolution" was merely a continuation of the scientific breakthroughs made by Catholics during many prior centuries.

It is often thought that the Enlightenment was generally against religion, but this assessment is incomplete; though the Enlightenment had its share of atheists and atheist-sympathizers, their enemy was not religion generally, but rather the Catholic faith specifically.[417] Though the fundamental basis for the Enlightenment was founded on a lie, it nevertheless gave its proponents and their listeners the impetus to discredit, distrust, and destroy the Catholic Church. That is no overstatement. Voltaire was perhaps the most influential Enlightenment thinker, and he commonly referred to the Catholic Church simply as "the infamous"; indeed, he ended his letters with the closing, "Écrasez l'infâme," which means "Crush the infamous."[418] More specifically, Voltaire aimed to crush the Catholic Church in France.

He nearly lived to see that goal accomplished in the bloodthirsty massacre of the French Revolution, during which thousands of Catholics were murdered, often by beheading at the guillotine. The government confiscated all the houses of Catholic religious orders; the Cathedral of Notre Dame was seized, desecrated, and offered to the "Goddess of Reason"; the calendar was officially changed to remove any reference to the birth of Jesus; and graveyard crosses were smashed and burned.[419] Some of the most wanton and deranged brutality seemed reserved for the Carmelites. The Carmelite house in Compiegne was turned into a prison, where priests were systematically executed in mock trials—if they had a trial at all.[420] The Carmelites nuns and their companions were given the option to either renounce their vows or be executed.

Undoubtedly drawing strength from the intercession of Teresa of Ávila, all affirmed their vows and were guillotined in their habits. Voltaire's "enlightened" soulmate, Denis Diderot, proclaimed, "Man will never be free until the last king is strangled with the entrails of the last priest."[421] The French Revolutionary mob surely tried to make that satanic nightmare come true. One might object to referencing the French Revolution as representative of the Enlightenment philosophy, yet the fact remains: although not all Enlightenment thinkers called for open violence against the Catholic Church, some certainly did just that.

Whether one believes that the natural consequence of the Enlightenment is political violence, it cannot be denied that the Enlightenment—in sum—is profoundly anti-Catholic; more to our purposes in this book, it is *anti-miracle*. Rationalism is a foundational principle of the Enlightenment; that is, there is the insistent belief that natural science can explain everything. Quite intentionally, their position leaves no room for supernatural events such as miracles. Brad Gregory explains:

> Newton's physics made possible an intellectually powerful conception of nature consisting of inviolable natural laws. Half a century earlier, Descartes's conception of the universe as a comprehensive mechanism of efficient causes was already interpretable as leaving no possibility for miracles. This is exactly how it was viewed by Spinoza. . . . Because Spinoza had on the basis of his own assumptions, definitions, and axioms assimilated God to nature, "which maintains an eternal, fixed, and immutable order," a belief in miracles "would be contrary to nature and its laws."[422]

In the words of seventeenth-century freethinker Charles Blount, "Whatever is against nature, is against *reason*; and whatever is against reason is *absurd*, and therefore also to be rejected and refuted," because *"all events happen according to the Eternal Order of Nature."*[423] Blount's is a highly telling statement, because it illustrates the reflexive and unshakable rejection of the stigmata by "enlightened" minds. From his perspective, "miracles" are to be "rejected and refuted," but never investigated according to scientific methods. David Gregory points out the irony, "Given the assumptions and endeavor of the modern natural sciences, the profound irony is that science precludes any possible verification of the claim that miracles worked by a transcendent God are impossible. Only a transgression of science understood as an empirical investigation of the natural world could rule out the possibility of miracles."[424] For that matter, it *was* a transgression of science to affirm miracles impossible in the first place. As Gregory points out, David Hume's "scornful repudiation of Christianity was a *premise* of his argument against miracles" [emphasis added]; in other words, he did not arrive at their rejection "based on science or reason"[425] but on predisposed opinion.

Despite the impossibility of scientifically proving miracles impossible, rationalists affirm that anyone who believes in the stigmata is clinging to the absurd—irrespective of what evidence he might think he has. This illustrates why insanity is the charge against everyone who claims to bear mystical stigmata and why insanity is the charge against everyone who claims to believe them. Worse, it also explains why stigmatists—and those who believe and promote them—are attacked. Enlightenment thinking remains a powerful influence in contemporary times. Catholics must understand this because the arguments against the stigmata are often not genuine; instead, they are false interrogatives that rest upon bias and intellectual prejudice.

HYSTERIA?

Faced with the fact that many saints have exhibited the wounds of Jesus, many skeptics, such as Donovan Rawcliffe, dismiss the stigmata as "hysteria."[426] In fairness to Rawcliffe, he was not alone in that assessment; the diagnosis is exceedingly common. This is absurd on several levels, beginning with the fact that hundreds of doctors have personally witnessed thousands of medically inexplicable wonders from the stigmatists for decades, and these accounts cannot simply be explained away with a charge of mental illness. But beyond that, the charge of *hysteria* has been remarkably unscientific for centuries, not to mention verifiably misogynistic—as we are about to examine. For these reasons, the term has almost completely fallen out of use in modern psychology. The fact that the term was ever used as a medical or psychological diagnosis has become an embarrassment for the profession. Since that does not prevent people from using the term *hysteria* in reference to the stigmatists, we will examine it here.

The term *hysteria* arrived in English from the Greek root word meaning *uterus*. Thus, whereas *hysterectomy* means to remove the uterus, *hysteria* literally means "a displacement of the uterus."[427] But somehow, hysteria came to be defined as "an uncontrollable outburst of emotion or fear, often characterized by irrationality, laughter, weeping, etc."[428] Word Origins.com asks a very natural question, "How did a Greek root referring to the uterus come to mean a state of overwhelming emotion? Through a combination of medieval medicine and many centuries of misogyny, that's how."[429] That understates things considerably.

The truth is that, for centuries, the diagnosis of "hysteria" led to widespread, institutionalized, and slanderous medical malpractice against women. As Anne P. DePrince writes in a 2023 *Psychology Today* article, "Throughout history, women's physical and psychological ailments have been labeled hysterical, and women blamed for their symptoms."[430] A research report appearing in *Clinical Practice & Epidemiology in Mental Health* notes, "Hysteria is undoubtedly the first mental disorder attributable to women."[431] The report further points out that Sigmund Freud regarded hysteria as "an exclusively female disease."[432] The prevailing medical theories about hysteria were that women are "vulnerable to mental disorders" and "easily influenced . . . by the 'supernatural.'"[433] The report illustrates that this attitude toward women amounted to a "pseudo-scientific prejudice."[434]

Aggravating that prejudice, when women came to doctors (or were brought to doctors), the physicians very often simply diagnosed them with hysteria.[435] Dr. R.W. Hynek—who spent considerable time and effort extensively documenting the stigmata of Therese Neumann—exposed this prejudice in 1932, writing, "In practice, in dealing with confused enigmatical cases where there is nothing upon which a diagnosis may be based, but where the doctor must say *something*, hysteria is the veritable *Deus ex machina* which saves his reputation."[436] Asti Hustvedt, author of *Medical Muses: Hysteria in Nineteenth-Century Paris*, writes that in the nineteenth century, hysteria served as "a medical 'trash can'—that is, the label where all medically inexplicable symptoms were dumped."[437] Given this bias and the reflexive diagnosis, coupled with the fact that the great majority of stigmatists in history have been women, is it any wonder that physicians unceremoniously dismissed stigmatists as hysterics?

Another fascinating aspect of this discussion of hysteria is the person of Jean-Martin Charcot (1825-1893). At the beginning of this chapter, we saw that Imbert-Gourbeyre accused Charcot of ignorance and dishonesty in diagnosing the stigmatists. Though his name is virtually unknown today outside psychiatric circles, Charcot was one of Europe's most powerful and influential doctors. He was the head physician at France's Salpêtrière hospital, which housed the female outcasts of society. Some might say *imprisoned* since many patients were never released; indeed, the Salpêtrière had once served as a prison.[438] During Charcot's administration, the Salpêtrière grew to five thousand patients, making it "the largest medical institution in Europe."[439]

The power and influence a person can gain in such a position is obvious; even beyond that, many accounts emphasize that he had an authoritarian rule, reflected in the fact that the press dubbed him the "Caesar of the Salpêtrière."[440] In fairness, it must be stated that Charcot did advance the science of neurology, as Imbert-Gourbeyre highlights. However, as Hustvedt notes, although neurology gained him respect, "it was hysteria that made him famous."[441] It also made him wealthy.[442] Throwing weekly parties for the Parisian rich and famous, Charcot was the real-life medical equivalent of the Great Gatsby. Charcot had it all except for an accurate understanding of what he called *hysteria.*[443]

An old saying is, "If your only tool is a hammer, all your problems look like nails." This *bon mot* could easily be applied to Charcot. The medical records illustrate that about a decade before Charcot arrived for an internship at the Salpêtrière, about 1 percent of patients were diagnosed with hysteria; by 1883, under Charcot's management, the number skyrocketed to greater than 20 percent.[444] Indeed, hysteria was a phantom pandemic of Charcot's own making.

Perhaps because he seemed more interested in *diagnosing* his patients than *healing* them,[445] some of Charcot's methods of treatment were particularly disturbing.* In nineteenth-century France, there may not have been "Big Pharma," but there was Big Charcot, who seemed insistent on administering drugs to his diagnosed hysteria patients. Hustvedt notes, "Not only were some of the medications administered at the Salpêtrière creating addicts, but many of the symptoms Charcot attributed to hysteria may very well have been side effects from the drugs used to treat it."[446] Another particularly distasteful method of "treatment" involved an "ovary compressor," which is described as "an apparatus that was attached to the patient's abdomen and worked like a vice grip to apply pressure to the hysterogenic zone in order to elicit or suppress a hysterical attack."[447]

While Charcot was alive, he had such a monopolistic stranglehold on the Parisian medical community that few physicians dared question him. Once he passed away, however, he faced plenty of justifiable derision—but not nearly enough, considering the damage he had done. By the 1920s, his former students were speaking openly about the fact that Charcot had been utterly wrong about his near-ubiquitous diagnoses of hysteria.[448]

In this context, the fact that Charcot casually accused stigmatic women of *hysteria* is entirely consistent with his own deranged thought process—one that has been discredited by his students who witnessed his "treatments" and re-

* Perhaps the most bizarre element of Charcot's "treatment" of these poor women was that he regularly exhibited them to French audiences—often in various states of undress while they posed in erotic positions and simulated sexual acts. Charcot had his share of contemporary critics of these shows, who recognized these shows not as something of medical value but a sadomasochistic perversion and victimization. Beyond the shows, Charcot issued a book of such pictures of these "hysterical" women that was widely circulated in France. Andrew Scull, *Hysteria: The Biography* (Oxford: Oxford University Press, 2009), 104, 119-124.

jected by contemporary psychologists and psychiatrists. The term has been stricken from the psychiatric lexicon. Though stigmatists will still be accused of hysteria, we must nevertheless recognize that hysteria is anti-science. It is a baseless, fruitless, and ignorant charge.

AUTOSUGGESTION

In addition to the charge of hysteria above, Donovan Rawcliffe posits that "autosuggestion" may very well account for the presence of the stigmata.[449] As with hysteria, this is a typical "explanation" for the stigmata. Just as he did not define *hysteria*, Rawcliffe does not define *autosuggestion*. But in 2021, a team of neurologists did an extensive study of autosuggestion for the journal titled *Experimental Brain Research*. They define autosuggestion as "instantiation and reiteration of ideas or concepts by oneself aiming to actively bias one's own perceptual, brain or interoceptive states, as well as the valence of perceived sensations."[450] A simple example of this would be "thinking of itching" and then feeling itchy.[451] The authors point out that autosuggestion is used with cognitive behavioral therapy—a mainstream practice that has succeeded in helping some people think more positively. As documented in numerous case studies, autosuggestion has also proven successful in pain management. To be sure, autosuggestion has real-world beneficial applications.

But for all autosuggestion's benefits, it has profound physical limitations. For instance, although an amputee might benefit from autosuggestion to address his phantom pains, it would be absurd to think autosuggestion could help him regrow a leg. The idea of the weekly manifestation of stigmatic wounds—followed by the immediate healing of those wounds—cannot be explained by autosuggestion. Nor can the ability to be nourished by the Eucharist alone for decades, nor the ability to discern holy objects, nor levitate, nor read minds, nor any of the other peripheral medically inexplicable powers of so many stigmatists.

What about the case of sweating blood, which, on rare cases, can naturally occur in moments of uncontrollable and superlative fear? Using the professional definition above, this is not autosuggestion. Why? Because as the doctors of neurology explain their meaning, "The word 'actively' indicates that autosuggestion is volitional and intentional, and links to concepts such as agency or free will." But the *sweating of blood as the result of horrifying fear* is not intentional. Apart from that, worrying oneself sick is one thing; worrying oneself to holes in his hands and feet, along with wounds in his head, shoulder, and side, is quite another.

There is the theory that some people love Jesus so much that they produce the stigmata upon meditating on his wounds. Fr. Charles M. Carty raises an interesting objection to this theory: if a powerful contemplation of Jesus' passion could produce stigmatic wounds, why didn't *all* the saints have the stigmata? It's a great question. Were saints such as Bernadette, Thérèse of Lisieux, Maximilian Kolbe, Vincent de Paul, John Vianney, and Mother Teresa somehow lacking in compassion for Christ? What about the Blessed Virgin Mary, St. John the apostle, and St. Mary Magdalene at the foot of the cross? At the risk of upsetting some ecumenical sensitivities, we might ask another question: where are the Protestant stigmatists? Undoubtedly, many Protestants deeply love Jesus, too. Where are the documented cases?

Speculations of this nature aside, if intensely compassionate love were sufficient to spontaneously produce corresponding wounds in the person loving, why would this not occur in other cases, such as when a mother mourns a wounded child, or a wife her husband lost in battle? Even though it is not the case, if love *of Jesus* were uniquely capable of producing this astonishing subjective phenomenon, it begs the question whether the skeptics are proving what they want to dismiss: the supernatural nature of the love in question.

DEMONIC STIGMATA?

Some have posited that the stigmata may be of demonic origin; even Imbert-Gourbeyre allowed for the possibility that demons *could* cause wounds if God allowed them to do so. Over the years, some people have latched on to this idea as the most likely explanation. That fact shouldn't surprise us. Even Jesus was accused of demonic association. The scene is described in Matthew's Gospel: "Then a blind and mute demoniac was brought to him, and he healed him, so that the mute man spoke and saw. And all the people were amazed, and said, 'Can this be the Son of David?' But when the Pharisees heard it they said, 'It is only by Be-el'zebul, the prince of demons, that this man casts out demons'" (12:22-24). This accusation of demonic influence remains even today. Of course, one of the most bizarre spiritual characteristics of the present age is the eagerness of people to believe in the power of the devil while simultaneously denying God.

As a response to the charge that stigmatic wounds are a demonic work, the response of Jesus to the Pharisees applies: "Every kingdom divided against itself is laid waste, and no city or house divided against itself will stand; and if Satan casts out Satan, he is divided against himself; how then will his kingdom stand?" (Matt. 12:25-26). Jesus provides us a further answer to this charge in his warning against false prophets:

> Beware of false prophets, who come to you in sheep's clothing but inwardly are ravenous wolves. You will know them by their fruits. Are grapes gathered from thorns, or figs from thistles? So, every sound tree bears good fruit, but the bad tree bears evil fruit. A sound tree cannot bear evil fruit, nor can a bad tree bear good fruit. Every tree that does not bear good fruit is cut down and thrown into the fire. Thus you will know them by their fruits (Matt. 7:15-20).

CONCLUSION

After a certain point, even many skeptics admit that the wounds of the stigmata—at least on the bodies of *some* stigmatists—are real. There is simply too much medical evidence conducted under controlled experimentation to conclude otherwise. Thus, as we have seen, wild theories of various forms of lunacy have developed, in a desperate attempt to find some explanation for these wounds other than the divine. Slander and libel would be unfair to anyone, but it is uniquely unfair to dismiss as lunatics men and women of towering intellects. Sainthood and stigmata aside, the prose of Catherine of Siena and Teresa of Ávila's beautiful writings occupy a revered place in the Western canon.

Rather than acknowledge the genius of these women stigmatists, though, the skeptics celebrate men like Charcot, who institutionalized sexual abuse of women by the thousand in the name of science. But though skeptics and their skepticism come and go, the stigmatists remain. From heaven, they continue to pray for the faithful. The next chapter will illustrate that they continue to work miracles on earth.

9

MORE POWERFUL THAN BEFORE: THE POSTHUMOUS MIRACLES OF THE STIGMATISTS

> Skeptical materialists who reject the mind of the Church have some very embarrassing facts to explain.
>
> —William Thomas Walsh[452]

When posthumous biographies are written about kings, movie stars, and great military leaders, the final chapters inevitably discuss how and when these persons died. In the hagiographies within this book, we have often done the same, introducing saints with the years of their births and deaths, for example, St. Margaret Mary Alacoque (1647-1690). But that fails to tell the whole story because, for the saint, the year of death is not the end. Though the soul departed from the body, the saint may still have work to do on earth from the vantage point of eternal life. Such was the case with many stigmatists.

In some sense, every human body—as with all the wonders of creation—expresses God's love, glory, and mercy. But in general, the body is somewhat opaque, not entirely transparent to what takes place in the soul. In a remarkably unique way, the bodies of the stigmatists magnificently reflect the love, mercy, and glory of God. So, although we cannot see the souls of the stigmatists—either on earth or in heaven—we can see their bodies, and these have been enough, in many cases, to catalyze conversions to the Catholic faith and the deepening of that faith. To continue that process of conversion, the bodies of some of the stigmatists have continued to exhibit miraculous wonders hundreds of years after their deaths. The principal miracle has been bodily *incorruptibility*—that is, miraculous preservation. In this chapter, we will investigate the nature of incorruptibility by looking at five female stigmatists in particular. We will also briefly discuss some of the miracles attributed to the intercession of these stigmatic saints.

As we will see, God is still working wonders through these stigmatists.

CORRUPTIBILITY V. INCORRUPTIBILITY

Many cultures in history have had some process of embalming, which is the preparation of a body for public or private viewing before burial. Generally, embalming preserves the body for a few days or even a few weeks. The details of the process can strike the squeamish as rather macabre and are not necessary to describe here, but the essential point is this: without embalming, the human body begins to stiffen with *rigor mortis* within hours, and it starts to decompose very quickly, accompanied by a horrible stench.[453] The Gospel of John illustrates this point. When Jesus indicates that he is going to raise Lazarus from the dead, Martha says, "Lord, by this time there will be an odor, for he has been dead four days" (John 11:39).

However, bodies cannot be indefinitely preserved even with the embalming process. The Egyptians tried it. As Joan Carroll Cruz, author of the definitive *The Incorruptibles*, points out, "Many Egyptian mummies have survived to modern times in remarkable states of preservation, as we know, but many were reduced to dust during scientific examinations or putrefied rapidly when the bandaging was removed."[454] Cruz also discusses the fact that some bodies can be "accidentally preserved" for a relatively longer time if the optimal conditions of aridity exist. Even in those rare cases, "the products of the deliberate and accidental preservations, without exception, have been not more than shriveled specimens, always rigid and extremely dry."[455] As Cruz explains, the incorruptible saints do not fall into either intentional or accidental preservation categories, but rather into a medically inexplicable one altogether.

ST. CLARE OF MONTEFALCO (D. 1308)

In 1881, over five and a half centuries after St. Clare of Montefalco's death, John Addington Symonds of *The Cornhill Magazine* wrote about his visit to Clare's coffin.[456] (The name "Clare" is the anglicized version of "Chiara," which is how Symonds refers to her here.) Here is his beautiful account of what he saw:

> Before us in the dim light there lay a woman covered with a black nun's dress. Only her hands, and the exquisitely beautiful pale outline of her face (forehead, nose, mouth, and chin, modelled in purest outline, as though the injury

> of death had never touched her), were visible. Her closed eyes seemed to sleep. She had the perfect peace. . . . I have rarely seen anything which surprised and touched me more. . . . Chiara's shrine was hung round with her relics; and among these the heart extracted from her body was suspended. Upon it, apparently wrought into the very substance of the mummied flesh, were impressed a figure of the crucified Christ, the scourge, and the five stigmata. . . . And I think now of this girl, as of a damsel of romance, a Sleeping Beauty in the wood of time."[457]

Reading these words, one must remind himself that Symonds is writing about a woman who bore the painful stigmata and died at about the age of forty, nearly 600 years earlier. Yet he seems to describe a transcendently beautiful woman in the bloom of youth who casually drifted off for a nap on a gentle summer afternoon. Beyond that, as Cruz notes, her body has never been stiff; instead, it is "still perfectly supple."[458] From a medical perspective, her body should have turned to dust long ago, yet there she lies—to the wonder of Symonds and the rest of Clare's visitors.

But though it may appear that Clare has been simply napping, quite the contrary is true: she has been interceding for the miracles of those who have asked for her prayers.

As a general principle, the Catholic Church requires that at least three miracles be clearly attributed to a person's intercession before he or she is canonized. That did not represent much of a hurdle for Clare's case. When the Sacred Congregation of Rites was assembling its investigation for Clare's canonization, they were presented with not three but thirty-five proposed miracles, of which they ultimately decided on six that they classified as "more eminent than the rest" and "beyond all doubt."[459]

The first miracle was the most obvious by far: Clare's heart. In chapter 3, we referenced Clare's deathbed assurance: "You will find the cross of Jesus graven on my heart."[460] When an autopsy was performed, she was proven correct. Her heart was significantly larger than average, but beyond that, it was imprinted with the signs of Jesus' passion. Fr. Lawrence Tardy describes:

> The figure of the Crucified was found in the right side of the heart, and that of the scourge in the center of the left; between both was the pillar, and at its foot the crown of thorns; at the right side of the figure of the Crucified were the three nails, and under them the lance; and at the left side of the same was the reed with the sponge.[461]

The other five miracles were "instantaneous and perfect" cures: *first*, the "monstrous" congenital disability of a boy named Cetto Speranza; *second*, the healing of the "inveterate lameness" and "other grave symptoms" of a young man named Antony Romanone; *third,* the prolapsed uterus of a woman named Flora Nicolai; *fourth,* the "cancer of the eyes, together with blindness, and an enormous wasting away of the eye-balls" of a child named Lucarello Jacometti; and *fifth,* a hernia of a cleric named Chino Rinalducci. The saint, dubbed "Sleeping Beauty," has been very active in her intercession from heaven, continuing to pray on behalf of her trusting friends on earth.

ST. RITA OF CASCIA (D. 1457)

St. Rita's body was never embalmed; the decomposition of her body should have proceeded rapidly. Yet, before Rita's beatification by Pope Urban VIII in 1627—one hundred and seventy-one years following her death—her body was exhumed, and it was discovered that she was incorrupt.[462] Beyond that, Rita's face appeared not to be that of a seventy-six-year-old woman but a young woman again. The wound on her forehead—which once emitted a revolting stench—now smelled like a flower garden.[463]

In 1682, a group of local dignitaries, including the vice-governor of Cascia, the captain of the infantry of Cascia, and the notary public of Cascia produced a written deposition, swearing to Rita's incorruptibility and her associated miracles. The deposition is worth quoting at length:

> On Saturday the 16th of May, 1682, in the church called anciently St. Mary Magdalen's, but now called B. Rita's, we the undersigned, of the territory of Cascia, diocese of Spoleto, by means of our oath, etc., in the presence of me a notary and Chancellor forane of the bishop of the territory of Cascia, give full and undoubted testimony . . . that at the present the blessed body of our B. Rita is entire, uncorrupted, with its flesh white, without any stain of corruption, with its eyes open, and especially the left, which is seen to be more open than the right, and with the eyelids separated, and with the mouth somewhat opened, in which are seen and very clearly distinguished the white teeth, the hands likewise white, etc. . . .
>
> Similarly we attest as above, that we have felt many times an odor and a fragrance wonderful and of Paradise, without being able to say what kind of odor it is, and this sometimes has been observed in a manner that it was felt outside the church. And by much more is this odor marvelous inasmuch as her body was not embalmed, or opened, but placed in the coffin where it is found, with all the internal portions not separated, nor divided from the body.

> Similarly we fully testify as above, that we have many times observed that her blessed body had raised itself from the place where ordinarily it lies up to the top of the little grating which is above the said coffin, where reposes the same blessed body, and especially this happens on the occurrence of her feast."[464]

The cases of Rita's "odor of sanctity," to use the terms of mystical theology, are so numerous and documented that they served as the first miracle for her canonization. Another miracle attributed to Rita involved healing a girl whose eyes had become disfigured and almost totally blind due to smallpox. Similarly to St. Rita, her wounds emitted a vile odor. Multiple doctors pronounced her case incurable, and the girl was sent to live with the Augustinian nuns of Cascia. While caring for her, one of the nuns had an idea: she touched a dress to the enclosed case of Rita and gave it to the girl to wear. The nuns also touched a piece of silver that had once touched Rita to the young girl's eyes. The girl was immediately cured.[465] Seeing what had occurred, a doctor in Rome took the following oath:

> It is a matter of conscience and of necessity to reiterate my opinion that this cure has been instantaneous, perfect, and lasting, in no way caused by art or by natural forces, impossible to take place except by miracle, which by science and by conscience must be classified with the great inexplicable portents which the Omnipotent God allows to be performed by his faithful servants, and in our case by Bl. Rita of Cascia; and this I again repeat in my deposition under my oath.[466]

ST. TERESA OF ÁVILA (D. 1582)

Rita was not the only stigmatist with the postmortem odor of sanctity. Historian William Thomas Walsh writes that when Teresa of Ávila died on October 4, "a sweet smell which nobody could describe or identify came from the body. . . . It became so overpowering in the cell where she died that the windows had to be opened to prevent headache and faintness."[467] That was only the beginning of miraculous wonders for the future Doctor of the Church, beginning with the fact that her body immediately looked younger.

Teresa was buried the next day in her habit without any embalming. For good measure, the grave was covered not only with dirt but with rocks and bricks. (The sisters had been concerned about someone taking the body as a relic. That was no idle worry. Teresa's holiness was well known in Spain, and it was, unfortunately, some Catholics' strange way of showing reverence for a body to steal it.) Nevertheless, when the sisters went to pray at her grave, they repeatedly noticed the unmistakable fragrance of her body. This went on for nine months, after which point the nuns requested the exhumation of her body. When the rocks, bricks, and dirt were finally uncovered, it was discovered that Teresa's coffin had been broken and filled with dirt, mold, and mildew. That environment was the perfect recipe for decay.

Cruz writes, "Moisture is the chief factor that encourages dissolution, yet many of the incorruptibles encountered this condition during their entombments, their preservations being inexplicably maintained in spite of it."[468] Teresa's body serves as a prime example. Teresa's body was covered in mud, but when the sisters cleaned her body, they saw what they very likely thought they would see: her body did not have the slightest decay. Beyond that, her body continued to emit a unique fragrance.[469] She was not put on display but instead reburied.[470] Two years after Teresa's death, her body was again examined. This time, two physicians examined the body and concluded that the body had preserved so well that natural science could not explain it.[471] Her body was also exhumed in 1603, 1616, and 1750. In 1760, her body was displayed to the public before re-entombment.[472] Once again, in 1914, her body was again exhumed. Her body remained incorrupt, still surrounded by her signature fragrance.[473] Her body was also noted to be incorrupt again in 2024.

As to the miracles attributed to the intercession of Teresa, they are too vast to catalog. For those who think that the Catholic Church has a system of casually canonizing saints based on limited information about their holiness or on poorly verified miracles, it is worth considering the following. In the process of gathering information for Teresa's beatification and subsequent canonization, there were approximately *sixty formal hearings* conducted over three decades in numerous cities, including Ávila, Salamanca, Cuerva, Toledo, Lisbon, and Valencia, in which over *one thousand witnesses testified*.[474] We previously discussed that the canonization process often takes centuries, but Teresa's miracles and her influence were so well known that seemingly every dignitary in Spain, as well as many luminaries in other countries—including the king of Poland, the king, queen, and princess of France, and the archduke of Austria—urged the pope to canonize their beloved incorruptible saint quickly.[475]

Twelve miracles were approved for Teresa's beatification by Pope Paul V. For her canonization a few years later, sixteen miracles were analyzed: three during her life, one at her death, and twelve posthumously.[476] In the ceremony of her canonization, Gregory XV infallibly and magnificently proclaimed:

> For the honor and glory of God and of the indivisible Trinity, the exaltation and increase of the Catholic faith, by the authority and omnipotence of the merciful God, Father, Son, and Holy Spirit, and of the blessed apostles, and by ours, with the unanimous consent and opinion of our venerable brothers of the Holy Roman Church, cardinals, patriarchs, archbishops, and bishops, assistants and residents of this Roman Curia: we determine, judge, and define that the Blessed Teresa, virgin of glorious memory, born in the city of Ávila, whose holiness, purity of soul, and other excellences, miracles, and virtues are sufficiently known to us, is a saint, glorious and praiseworthy. Therefore, we decree and establish, define, and determine that she should be placed, enrolled, and numbered in the catalog and list of holy virgins, in the manner that, by the tenor of these presents, we place, write, and enlist her; and for this reason, all the faithful of Christ must revere, venerate, and regard her as a true saint, and as such, we command, desire, and order that she be held and revered.[477]

CONCLUSION

In a letter dated August 22, 2024, Bishop James V. Johnston stated, "The Catholic Church does not have an official protocol for determining if a deceased person's body is incorrupt, and incorruptibility is not considered to be an indication of sainthood."[478] That is true. There is no official formula for determining what constitutes miraculous incorruptibility. Further, incorruptibility alone is not decisive in determining a person's citizenship of heaven.

The same may be said of the stigmata phenomenon itself: there is no universal protocol for determining the mystical stigmata, nor does the presence of medically inexplicable stigmata alone guarantee sainthood. That is why the scope of this book has been on those men and women who have exhibited the stigmata *and* been canonized or at least beatified. The Catholic Church has infallibly canonized men and women who displayed the stigmata. Nevertheless, the Catholic Church does not *mandate* belief in the mystical stigmata—even the stigmata of Francis of Assisi—just as it does not mandate belief in Marian apparitions.

We live in an age in which we Catholics are almost ashamed of miracles, lest we embarrass ourselves in front of the smart kids at the front of the class: the free-thinkers, the scientists who practice scientism, and so forth. We should respond with wonder and delight that God loves us enough to send us visible miracles. And in this regard, there is no better way to conclude our discussion here to turn to our friend, Antoine Imbert-Gourbeyre. Years ago, he counseled and reminded the Catholic faithful of something very beautiful: "Miracles are jewels with which God delights in adorning great souls, his spouses, and his chosen ones, to show his power and glorify his mercy. If they are not always imposed on our faith, they are nonetheless a source of teaching and comfort. And then, when one loves their mother, why lay an irreverent hand on her to strip away some of her ornaments?"[479] We should allow Imbert-Gourbeyre's words to inspire us, and proclaim the beauty of the stigmatists.

EPILOGUE: WHAT THE STIGMATISTS STILL TEACH US

Very early in my research and in writing this book, I realized I could never look upon a crucifix the same way again. The great majority of artists' renderings of Jesus on the cross are sanitized, albeit for understandable reasons. Yet, that sanitization bothered me, because it failed to tell the whole story. Ultimately, however, I came to accept these representations; after all, no work of art can do justice to the real passion and crucifixion of Jesus. But that is where the stigmatists come in. The stigmatists give us an intense vision of his passion.

As this book has attempted to illustrate, the stigmatists over the centuries have helped us grow in both understanding and appreciation of the stigmata borne by Christ. When pilgrims went to visit Padre Pio or St. Lutgarde or St. Francis, they saw a living representation of Christ. These saints bore the stigmata, not so that they would be noticed, but that Jesus would be. These stigmatists not only preached the Gospel, but bore it on their bodies and souls. If we tell their stories today, the stigmatists can still bring pilgrims to grace. As I wrote, I felt them spiritually lifting me, and I needed their help. We all do.

The Crucifixion, and what it means for every soul on earth, is not easy to accept. Most Protestants have jettisoned the corpus of Christ, opting instead for a bare cross. But what is the cross without Christ? And if we envision a cross without Christ, where does that leave us? In some ways, I found myself asking that question as I wrote this book. Over the past few years, I have often said a silent prayer throughout the day: "Dear Jesus, please hold me close to your Sacred Heart, and never let me go." As I wrote this book, I continued to say the prayer, but it made me frightened as I said it while staring at the crucifix. *After all*, I worried, *Jesus is on the cross. Holding me close to his Sacred Heart would put me on the cross.*

Precisely.

I must desire to be held so close to Christ that I can feel and hear his Sacred Heart beat with love for me—whether he is in the cradle or on the cross.

The stigmatists showed us that when we unite our sufferings with Christ, we mystically enter into his passion. Simon of Cyrene was the first to help Jesus carry his cross, but he was not the last. St. Clare of Montefalco mystically embraced the cross, but in some sense—all Christians who unite their sufferings with Christ do so. In the garden of Gethsemane, Jesus foresaw all the sins of mankind, but he was certainly consoled by the knowledge that some would love him to the end in final perseverance. Surely, to follow Christ is to suffer *for* Christ, but it is to suffer *with* Christ at my side. That is an overwhelming consolation.

The modern world forms a phony dichotomy between suffering and happiness, but the stigmatists provide a biographical correction of that notion. Even in suffering, to know and love Jesus is to know profound happiness, fulfillment, and peace. That is what the stigmatists still teach us. It is not suffering with Jesus that causes misery; rather, it is separation from Jesus. The stigmatists knew suffering; they did not know separation. They lived happy. They died happy.

Precious few of the Catholic faithful are called to bear the wounds of Christ, yet all of us are called to kneel at the foot of the cross. Thus, to understand the meaning of the stigmata most richly, and to incorporate their most valuable lessons in our daily lives, we must turn to Mary, the Mother of God. The Blessed Virgin Mary did not endure the physical stigmata of her divine Son, yet she witnessed his passion and death. Considering her maternal and spiritual proximity to Jesus, her internal sufferings must have exceeded the physical pain of any of the stigmatists. This suffering seems foreshadowed in prophecy of Simeon, who predicted that a "sword will pierce through" her "soul" (Luke 2:35). We might say that Mary experienced the mystical stigmata of the soul. And although it is quite impossible to fully comprehend, Mary consoled the Second Person of the Trinity in his suffering. We must remember that Mary is our consolation as well.

What is more, she is our mother.

From the cross, Jesus uttered seven statements, and among them was one that applied to the whole world until the end of time—and in eternity: "Behold thy mother." In rejecting the sufferings that God allows us—that is, in refusing to carry our crosses—we are refusing to behold our mother—with tragic effects. As Fr. George Rutler writes, "When the criterion for reality is comfort, sensually or intellectually, the world becomes a more comfortable place. It also becomes an orphanage. The cross disappears, but vanishing with it is the woman who stood by it."[480] The stigmatists exhibited a beautiful devotion to Mary, and so must we. A devotion to Mary is the way to find our true home. As Fr. Rutler phrased it, "If souls attain heaven by becoming children, then they attain heaven by locating their mother."[481]

All the stigmatists in heaven, *pray for us.*

Mother of Perpetual Help, *pray for us.*

ABOUT THE AUTHOR

John Clark is a regular columnist for the *National Catholic Register* and has served as a speechwriter for candidates for the U.S. House, Senate, and president. He has written three books and more than 500 articles about Catholic family life and apologetics. John and his wife, Lisa, have nine children and live in central Florida.

ENDNOTES

1 *Mere Christianity* (HarperCollins), 52, Kindle.
2 *Modern Catholic Dictionary* (Garden City, NY: Doubleday & Company, 1980), 520.
3 *Parents of the Saints* (Gastonia, NC: TAN Books, 2020), loc. 150 of 7497, Kindle.
4 *A Doctor at Calvary: The Passion of Our Lord Jesus Christ as Described by a Surgeon*, trans. the Earl of Wicklow (n.p.: Muriwai Books, 2017), loc. 114 of 3936, Kindle.
5 Will Self, "Gospel is Sheer Torture," *The Standard*, 10 April 2012, https://www.standard.co.uk/culture/film/gospel-is-sheer-torture-7438233.html.
6 Jonathan Rosenbaum, "The Passion of the Christ," *Chicago Reader*, March 3, 1993, https://jonathanrosenbaum.net/2023/11/the-passion-of-the-christ/.
7 Martin Hengel, *Crucifixion*, trans. John Bowden (Philadelphia: Fortress Press, 1977), loc. 671 of 2463, Kindle. See also Woodrow Michael Kroll, *Roman Crucifixion and the Death of Jesus* (Eugene, OR: Resource Publications, 2023), 118-25, Kindle.
8 Ibid., loc. 671 of 2463. Italics in original.
9 Ibid., loc. 667 and 1527 of 2463.
10 Ibid., loc. 1433 of 2463. Italics in original.
11 *Against Verres*, ed. C.D. Yonge, Perseus Digital Library, https://www.perseus.tufts.edu/hopper/text?doc=Perseus%3Atext%3A1999.02.0018%3Atext%3DVer.%3Aactio%3D2%3Abook%3D5.
12 *The Spartacus War* (New York: Simon & Schuster, 2009), 205, Kindle.
13 Hengel, *Crucifixion*, loc. 1517 of 2463.
14 Ibid., loc. 1438 of 2463.
15 *The Spartacus War*, 17.
16 Ibid., 203.
17 Hengel, *Crucifixion*, loc. 1535 of 2463.
18 Ibid., loc. 1522 of 2463.
19 Ibid., loc. 706 of 2463.
20 *Man's Search for Meaning* (New York: Washington Square Press, 1984 edition), 106.
21 Kroll, *Roman Crucifixion*, 271.
22 Online Etymology Dictionary, v.s. "scourge," accessed August 10, 2024, https://www.etymonline.com/search?q=scourging.
23 *The Wars of the Jews*, bk. 1, ch. 2, sec. 4., ed. William Whiston, Perseus Digital Library, https://www.perseus.tufts.edu/hopper/text?doc=Perseus:text:1999.01.0148.

24 Ibid., bk. 6, ch. 5, sec. 3.
25 Kroll, *Roman Crucifixion*, 278.
26 *Church History* 15.4, trans. Arthur Cushman McGiffert, in *Nicene and Post-Nicene Fathers, Second Series*, vol. 1, ed. Philip Schaff and Henry Wace (Buffalo, NY: Christian Literature Publishing Co., 1890).
27 Barbet, *A Doctor at Calvary*, loc. 1033 of 3936, Kindle.
28 Hengel, *Crucifixion*, loc. 793 of 2463.
29 Strauss, *The Spartacus War*, 205-6. See also Hengel, *Crucifixion*, loc. 706 of 2463.
30 *A Doctor at Calvary*, loc. 1033 of 3936.
31 Ibid., loc. 122 of 3936. We might add that Barbet's comments affirm the overall value of the writings of the Fathers of the Church. Scripture sometimes gives us a peek, but only a peek, at incidents in the life and death of Jesus. The writings of the early Christians are irreplaceably important to deeply understand Christianity.
32 *Commentary on the Luke*, as cited in Aquinas, *Catena Aurea*, Luke 22:44 (Oxford: James Parker and Co., 1874).
33 *In Lucam* VI.xxii.44 (CCSL 120), as cited in Aquinas, *Catena Aurea*, Luke 22:44.
34 Andrew Edward Breen, *A Harmonized Exposition of the Four Gospels*, vol. 4 (Rochester, NY: John P. Smith Printing Company, 1908), 352.
35 *Exposition on Psalm* 141, as cited in Aquinas, *Catena Aurea*, Luke 22:44.
36 *The History of Animals*, trans. D'Arcy Wentworth Thompson http://classics.mit.edu/Aristotle/history_anim.3.iii.html. See also Breen, Harmonized Exposition, 4:350.
37 H.R. Jerajani, B. Jaju, M.M. Phiske, and N. Lade, "Hematohidrosis—A Rare Clinical Phenomenon," *Indian Journal of Dermatology* 54, no. 3 (July 2009): 290-92, https://pmc.ncbi.nlm.nih.gov/articles/PMC2810702/.
38 Breen, *Harmonized Exposition*, 4:350.
39 Jerajani, et al., "Hematohidrosis."
40 Ibid.
41 Ibid.
42 Elvira Mora and Javier Lucas, "Hematidrosis: Blood Sweat," *Blood* 121, no. 9 (2013):1493, https://doi.org/10.1182/blood-2012-09-450031.
43 H.T. Nguyen, P.T.D. Vo, T.T.D. Nguyen, Q.T. Nguyen, and D.L. Truong, "Hematohidrosis Induced by Separation Anxiety Disorder during COVID-19 Quarantine: A Case Report and Brief Literature Review," *Dermatol Reports* 15, no. 2 (December 2022):9615, doi: 10.4081/dr.2023.9615.
44 *The Dolorous Passion of Our Lord Jesus Christ* (Rockford, IL: TAN Books and Publishers, 1983), 134-35.
45 Ibid., 137.
46 As to the illegality of the trial itself, see Lord Shaw of Dunfermline, *The Trial of Jesus Christ* (London: George Newnes Limited, 1929), 21-23. See also John E. Richards, *The Illegality of the Trial of Jesus* (New Orleans: Chas E. George, 1914), 5-26.
47 Richards, *The Illegality of the Trial of Jesus*, 15.
48 Emmerich, *Dolorous Passion*, 156.
49 *https*://www.johnsanidopoulos.com/2019/04/history-of-relic-of-crown-of-thorns.html; *see also Gregory of Tours: Glory of the Martyrs*, trans. Raymond Van Dam (Liverpool: Liverpool University Press, 1988), 27.

50 John Sanidopoulos, "History and Authenticity of the Relic of the Crown of Thorns," April 18, 2019, *Orthodox Christianity Then and Now, https://*www.johnsanidopoulos.com/2019/04/history-of-relic-of-crown-of-thorns.html. See also Candace Sutton, "The Real Story of Jesus Christ's Crown of Thorns," April 20, 2019, *News.com.au*, https://www.news.com.au/lifestyle/real-life/news-life/the-real-story-of-jesus-christs-crown-of-thorns/news-story/ec56fd4a5016c533aabcc08e8bcdd72d.
51 Sutton, "The Real Story of Jesus Christ's Crown of Thorns," April 20, 2019.
52 Vincent Ferrer, "Sermon on Good Friday," accessed August 10, 2024, https://www.svfsermons.org/A724_Good%20Friday.htm. In his book, *A Doctor at Calvary*, Barbet attributes this quote to St. Vincent of Lèrins, but the quote is actually from St. Vincent Ferrer. Barbet also puts the number of thorns at seventy, but St. Vincent places it precisely at 72. See also "The Wrong St. Vincent," accessed August 10, 2024, https://medievalshroud.com/the-wrong-st-vincent/.
53 "Why Do Head Injuries Bleed So Much?" *University of Utah Health*, November 17, 2016, https://healthcare.utah.edu/healthfeed/2016/11/.
54 Barbet, *A Doctor at Calvary*, loc. 2500 of 3936. Barbet highlights this point.
55 Ibid., loc. 2500 of 3936.
56 Ibid., loc. 2507 of 3936. Emphasis in original.
57 *Crucifixion*, 1577.
58 *The Roman Martyrology* (Baltimore: John Murphy & Co., 1916), 340.
59 Ibid., 254.
60 Ibid., 298.
61 *The Stigmata and Modern Science* (Charlotte: TAN Books, 2013), loc. 30 of 423, Kindle.
62 *The Glory of Christendom* (Front Royal, Virginia: Christendom Press, 1993), 191-92.
63 *Summa Theologiæ*, I-II:32:8.
64 William R. Cook and Ronald B. Herzman, "Great Courses: Francis of Assisi," *Audible*, Lecture 1: 16:45—17:52.
65 "The Bull of Canonization of St. Francis of Assisi: Mira Circa Nos," August 14, 1228, *EWTN.com*, https://www.ewtn.com/catholicism/library/bull-of-canonization-of-st-francis-of-assisimira-circa-nos-7860.
66 P. Robinson, "St. Francis of Assisi," *The Catholic Encyclopedia* (New York: Robert Appleton Company, 1909). Francis's baptismal name was Giovanni, but he was renamed Francesco by his parents.
67 *The Life of St. Francis of Assisi* 1.1 (Charlotte, NC: Saint Benedict Press, 2010).
68 Bonaventure, *Life of St. Francis* 1.5; Robinson, "St. Francis of Assisi."
69 "A History of Leprosy, The Debilitating Disease of Separation," *Medical Daily*, May 13, 2015, https://www.medicaldaily.com/history-leprosy-debilitating-disease-separation-photos-332998.
70 *Life of St. Francis* 1.5.
71 Bonaventure, *Life of St. Francis* 6.9.
72 *Life of St. Francis* 6.9.
73 Bonaventure, *Life of St. Francis* 5.4.
74 Ibid., 5.4.
75 Ibid., 2.8.

76 Ibid., 6.4.
77 Ibid., 3.10.
78 Ibid. 6.5.
79 Candide Chalippe, *The Life and Legends of Saint Francis of Assisi*, ed. Hilarion Duerk (New York: P.J. Kenedy & Sons, 1918), 354.
80 *The Writings of St. Francis of Assisi*, trans. Benen Fahy (London: Burns & Oates, 1964), 78-79.
81 Ibid., 79.
82 Ibid., 101.
83 *Life of St. Francis* 1.5. Emphasis added.
84 Johannes Jorgensen, *Saint Francis of Assisi: A Biography* (New York: Longmans, Green, and Co., 1912), 42.
85 Ibid., 298.
86 *Writings*, 140.
87 *The Five Wounds of Saint Francis* (Charlotte, NC: TAN Books, 2011), 166-67, Kindle.
88 Introduction to *The Writings of St. Francis of Assisi*, trans. Pascal Robinson (original pub. 1905; repub. London: Forgotten Books, 2007), 2.
89 "La Verna in Casentino," *Discover Tuscany*, accessed August 11, 2024, https://discovertuscany.com/casentino/la-verna.html.
90 Regis J. Armstrong, J.A. Wayne Hellmann, and William J. Short, eds., *Francis of Assisi: Early Documents* (New York: New City Press, 2023), 226-27.
91 *First Life of St. Francis of Assisi*, trans. Christopher Stace (London: Society for Promoting Christian Knowledge, 2000), 93-94.
92 Armstrong et al., *Francis of Assisi: Early Documents*, 227.
93 *First Life*, 96.
94 Ibid., 96.
95 Benfatti, *Five Wounds*, 60, 152.
96 Ibid., 152, 172.
97 This translation, by Kajetan Esser and Duane Lapsanski, is the fruit of their work based on the original manuscript. Cited in Armstrong, *Francis of Assisi: Early Documents*, 108-9.
98 *Writings*, 124.
99 *Life of St. Francis* 13.4.
100 Jorgensen, *Saint Francis of Assisi*, 301.
101 *Five Wounds*, 35.
102 Ibid., 107.
103 *Life of St. Francis* 13.8.
104 Jorgensen, *Saint Francis of Assisi*, 305. See also Carroll, *Glory of Christendom*, 204.
105 Ibid., 13.8.
106 Tom Gurney, "Giotto," *TheHistoryOfArt.org*, June 19, 2020, https://www.thehistoryofart.org/giotto/death-of-st-francis/.
107 *Glory of Christendom*, 205.
108 "Mystical Stigmata," *The Catholic Encyclopedia* (New York: Robert Appleton, 1912).
109 *Saint Lydwine of Schiedam: 1380-1433*, trans. Agnes Hastings (Charlotte, NC: TAN Books, 1979), 59, Kindle.
110 Ibid., 37.

111 Ibid., 37-56.
112 Ibid., 76.
113 Ibid., 68.
114 A. Poulain, "Mystical Stigmata," *The Catholic Encyclopedia.*
115 John Ayto, *Bloomsbury Dictionary of Word Origins* (London: Bloomsbury Publishing, 2001), 193.
116 A. Poulain, "Ecstasy," *The Catholic Encyclopedia* (New York: Robert Appleton, 1912).
117 Ibid.
118 *The Life of St. Lutgarde*, trans. Mark Reynolds (no city or date indicated), 41-42, Kindle.
119 Ibid., 43.
120 Ibid.
121 *The Enigma of the Stigmata*, trans. P.J. Hepburne-Scott (New York: Hawthorn Books, 1962), 55-56.
122 Larry Peterson, "Servant of God; Maria Domenica Lazzeri—The Last 14 Years of Her Life She Ate Nothing Except for Receiving Holy Communion," *Catholic 365*, July 27, 2018, https://www.catholic365.com/article/9138/.
123 Johann Joseph von Gorress, *The Stigmata: A History of Various Cases*, ed. H. Austin (London: Thomas Richardson and Son, 1883), 73. See also Deacon Albert E. Graham. *The Stigmata: Those Who Bore the Wounds of Christ* (No city of publication listed: Trafford Publishing, 2023), 280, Kindle. See also Biot, *Enigma of the Stigmata*, 56.
124 Ibid., 140.
125 *The Anne Catherine Emmerich Collection* (London: Catholic Way Publishing, 2019), loc. 566 of 61550, Kindle.
126 Reverend Germanus, *The Life of Saint Gemma Galgani*, trans. A.M. O'Sullivan (original pub. 1913; repub. Aeterna Press, 2015), 52, Kindle.
127 Biot, *Enigma*, 28.
128 Alban Butler, *Butler's Lives of the Saints: Complete Edition*, ed. Herbert Thursdon (Omaha: Patristic Publishing, 2019), 1912, Kindle.
129 *The Life of St. Mary Frances of the Five Wounds of Jesus Christ* (Dublin: M. H. Gill, 1878), 114.
130 Joseph Sicardo, *St. Rita of Cascia: Saint of the Impossible*, trans. Dan J. Murphy (Charlotte, NC: TAN Books, 1990), 109-10, Kindle.
131 Richard Connolly, *Life of St. Rita of Cascia* (London: R. & T. Washbourne, 1903), 134. See also Butler, Lives, 2591.
132 Richard Stracke, "St. Rita of Cascia: The Iconography," accessed August 11, 2024, https://www.christianiconography.info/staMariaAngeli/stRita.html.
133 Sicardo, *St. Rita of Cascia*, 111.
134 Gorress, *Stigmata*, 27, 72-73.
135 A Sister of the Congregation of St. Catharine of Siena, *Short Lives of the Dominican Saints*, ed. Fr. Proctor (London: Kegan Paul, Trench, Trubner & Co., 1901), 6-7.
136 E. Bougard, *Life of Saint Margaret Mary Alacoque* (New York, Benziger Brothers, 1920), 183.
137 Ibid., 183.
138 Ibid.

139 Omer Englebert, *The Lives of the Saints*, trans. Christopher and Anne Fremantle (New York: Barnes & Noble Books, 1994), 468.
140 Pope Francis, "Celebrata Dal Santo Padre Francesco Con Il Rito Della Canonizzazione," May 17, 2015, https://www.vatican.va/news_services/liturgy/libretti/2015/20150517-libretto-canonizzazione.pdf.
141 "St. Miriam of Jesus Crucified," Discalced Carmelite Friars: Washington Province of the Immaculate Heart of Mary, accessed August 12, 2024, https://www.discalcedcarmel.org/st-miriam-of-jesus-crucified.
142 Ibid.
143 F.M. Capes, *St. Catherine De' Ricci: Her Life, Her Letters, Her Community* (London: Burns & Oates, n.d.), v.
144 Ibid., 84.
145 Ibid.
146 Ibid., 272.
147 *The Diary of St. Veronica Giuliani: A Compendium*, trans. and ed. Bret Thoman (n.p.: Icona Press, 2023), 78, Kindle. All subsequent quotes in this paragraph refer this text, pages 78-79.
148 Ibid., 79.
149 *Life of St. Francis* 13.3.
150 *The Physical Phenomena of Mysticism*, ed. J.H. Crehan (Chicago: Henry Regnery Company, 1952), 48-49.
151 Butler, *Lives*, 114.
152 Gorress, *Stigmata*, 115-16.
153 Butler, *Lives*, 5739-5740. See also Georgiana Fullerton, *The Life of St. Frances of Rome, and Others* (London: Burns and Lambert, 1855), 156-57, Kindle.
154 Fullerton, *Life of St. Frances*, 159.
155 Ibid., 159.
156 *Dukes and Poets in Ferrara: A Study in the Poetry, Religion and Politics of the Fifteenth and Early Sixteenth Centuries* (London: Archibald Constable & Co., 1904), 466.
157 Fullerton, *Life of St. Frances*, 159. See also Butler, Lives, 5741.
158 Ibid., 160.
159 Ibid., 162.
160 Ibid.
161 "Blessed Marguerite Bays, Lay Mystic and Stigmatic," *Mystics of the Church*, accessed August 12, 2024, https://www.mysticsofthechurch.com/2015/02/blessed-marguerite-bays-lay-mystic-and.html.
162 Capes, *St. Catherine De' Ricci*, 82.
163 Cited in Thurston, *Physical Phenomena*, 55-56.
164 Biot, *Enigma*, 42.
165 *A Doctor at Calvary*, loc. 2405 of 3936.
166 Ibid., loc. 2354 of 3936.
167 Ibid.
168 Gilbert Dolan, *St. Gertrude the Great* (Omaha: Patristic Publishing, 2000), 9, Kindle.
169 Ibid., 11.
170 Mary Francis Cusack, *The Life and Revelations of Saint Gertrude* (Omaha: Patristic Publishing, 2021), 36-38, Kindle.

ENDNOTES

171 Lawrence Tardy, *Life of Saint Clare of Montefalco, Professed Nun of the Order of Hermits of Saint Augustine* (n.p.: Benzinger Brothers, 1884), 17-18, online version, https://archive.org/details/life-of-saint-clare-of-montefalco-by-father-lawrence-tardy/. Subsequent details in this paragraph from pages 18-22.
172 Ibid., 45-49.
173 Ibid., 49-50.
174 Ibid., 50.
175 Ibid., 52-53.
176 William Lloyd, *Saints of 1881* (London: Burns & Oates, 1882), 12.
177 Ibid., 17.
178 Tardy, *Life of Saint Clare*, 155.
179 Lloyd, *Saints*, 19.
180 *The Life of St. Catherine of Siena*, trans. George Lamb (New York: P J. Kennedy & Sons, 1960).
181 Ibid., 175.
182 Ibid., 176.
183 *The Life of St. Teresa of Ávila by Herself*, trans. J.M. Cohen (n.p.: Penguin Classics, 1988), 210, Kindle.
184 Ibid.
185 Ibid.
186 Thurston, *Physical Phenomena*, 67-68.
187 *St. Charles of Sezze: Autobiography*, ed. and trans. Leonard Perotti (London: Burns & Oates, 1963), 148.
188 Ibid., 149.
189 "Daniel Hale Williams and the First Successful Heart Surgery," *Columbia Surgery*, accessed August 12, 2024, https://columbiasurgery.org/news/daniel-hale-williams-and-first-successful-heart-surgery.
190 Butler, *Lives*, 3470.
191 *Diary of St. Veronica*, 21.
192 Ibid., 24.
193 Ibid., 25.
194 Francesco Castelli, *Padre Pio Under Investigation: The Secret Vatican Files* (San Francisco: Ignatius Press, 2008), 59, Kindle.
195 Biot, *Enigma*, 26.
196 Capes, *St. Catherine De' Ricci*, 83.
197 Robert P. Maloney, "The Beautiful Acarie," *Vincentiana* 41, no. 3, art. 7, https://via.library.depaul.edu/cgi/viewcontent.cgi?article=1989&context=vincentiana.
198 Covelle Newcomb, *Brother Zero: A Story of the Life of Saint John of God* (New York: Dodd, Mead & Company, 1959), 182.
199 *Les stigmatisées*, vol. 1: *Louise Lateau de Bois-D'Haine* (Paris: Victor Palme, 1873), i. All translations are mine.
200 "A Contribution to the Critique of Hegel's Philosophy of Right," *Works of Karl Marx 1843*, accessed August 12, 2024, https://www.marxists.org/archive/marx/works/1843/critique-hpr/intro.htm.
201 Helmut Gernsheim, *The History of Photography* (London: Thames and Hudson, 1969), 80.

202 Tine Van Osselaer, "The 'Affair of the Photographs': Controlling the Public Image of a Nineteenth-Century Stigmatic," *The Journal of Ecclesiastical History* 68, no. 4 (2017):784-806, doi:10.1017/S0022046917000665.
203 Gerald Molloy, *A Visit to Louise Lateau* (London: Burns, Oates, and Co., 1873), 35-37.
204 Cited in Imbert-Gourbeyre, *Les stigmatisées*, 1:1-2.
205 Ibid., 1:12.
206 *A Visit to Louise Lateau*, 40-41.
207 *Louise Lateau: The Ecstatica of Bois D'Haine*, trans. J.S. Shepard (London: Thomas Richardson & Son, 1872), 45. Italics in original.
208 *Louise Lateau*, 24-25. All quotes in this paragraph are from this same source.
209 Lefebvre, *Louise Lateau*, 26. All citations in this paragraph from the same source.
210 *Louise Lateau*, 72. Italics mine.
211 *A Visit to Louise Lateau*, 26.
212 Ibid., 26.
213 *Louise Lateau*, 27.
214 Ibid., 28.
215 *A Visit to Louise Lateau*, 52.
216 All references in this paragraph from *Louise Lateau*, 28-30.
217 Molloy, *A Visit to Louise Lateau*, 54.
218 *Louise Lateau*, 30.
219 Ibid., 31.
220 Ibid.
221 Ibid., 34.
222 Ibid., 34-35.
223 Ibid., 35.
224 Ibid.
225 Ibid., 36.
226 Ibid., 36-37.
227 Ibid., 40.
228 Ibid.
229 Ibid.
230 Ibid., footnote on pages 42-43.
231 Imbert-Gourbeyre, *Les stigmatisées*, 1:57.
232 Lefebvre, *Louise Lateau*, 42.
233 Ibid., 45.
234 Imbert-Gourbeyre, *Les stigmatisées*, 1:20.
235 Theodore G. Obenchain, *Genius Belabored: Childbed Fever and the Tragic Life of Ignaz Semmelweis* (Tuscaloosa: The University of Alabama Press, 2016), 24.
236 "Dr. Semmelweis's Biography," Semmelweis Society International, accessed August 12, 2024, https://web.archive.org/web/20190722212057/http://semmelweis.org/about/dr-semmelweis-biography/.
237 Obenchain, *Genius Belabored*, 162.
238 Sonja Schreiner, "Ignaz Semmelweis: A Victim of Harassment?" *Wien Med Wochenschr* 170, nos. 11-12 (2020):293-302, doi: 10.1007/s10354-020-00738-1. See also "Dr. Semmelweis's Biography," Semmelweis Society International.
239 *Semmelweis: His Life and His Doctrine* (Manchester: University of Manchester Publications), 2.

240 Imbert-Gourbeyre, *Les stigmatisées*, 1:viii.
241 Lefebvre's book that is repeatedly referenced in this chapter is the English version, published in 1872; however, the original French edition was published in 1869.
242 *Les stigmatisées*, 1:55.
243 Ibid., 1:39–40.
244 Ibid., 1:199.
245 Ibid., 1:43.
246 Ibid., 1:198.
247 Ibid., 1:34.
248 John Clark, "The Heavenly Beauty of Wedding Rings," National Catholic Register, October 17, 2024.
249 *Les stigmatisées*, 1:143.
250 Ibid., 1:143.
251 John Clark, "The Heavenly Beauty of Wedding Rings," National Catholic Register, October 17, 2024.
252 *Les stigmatisées*, 1:144.
253 Ibid., 1:144.
254 Ibid., 1:216.
255 Tine Van Osselaer, "Stigmata, Prophecies, and Politics: Louise Lateau in the German and Belgian Culture Wars of the Late Nineteenth Century," *Journal of Religious History* 42, no. 4 (December 2018): 591-610, https://doi.org/10.1111/1467-9809.12545.
256 "Louise Lateau: The Stigmatist," *The New York Times*, May 18, 1879.
257 *Les stigmatisées*, 1:218.
258 *Saint Lydwine of Schiedam*, 59.
259 *Diary of Saint Maria Faustina Kowalska: Divine Mercy in My Soul* (Stockbridge, Marian Press, 2005), no. 7.
260 Ibid., no. 9.
261 Ibid., no. 10.
262 Ibid., nos. 47–48.
263 Ibid., no. 1567.
264 Ibid., nos. 1588, 1605.
265 Ibid., no. 759.
266 Ibid., no. 759.
267 Ibid., no. 1425.
268 Ibid., no. 487.
269 Ibid., no. 70.
270 Ibid., no. 73.
271 Castelli, *Padre Pio Under Investigation*, loc. 1681 of 4655.
272 Bret Thoman, *The Life of Padre Pio of Pietrelcina: Mystery, Miracles, and Mission* (n.p.: Icona Press, 2024), loc. 1236 of 1895, Kindle.
273 Biot, *Enigma*, 41.
274 Thoman, *Life of Padre Pio*, loc. 1560 of 1895.
275 Ibid., loc. 1355 of 1895.
276 Ibid., loc. 1332 of 1895.
277 Ibid., loc. 1370 of 1895.
278 Ibid., loc. 1370–85 of 1895.

279 Ibid., loc. 1385 of 1895.
280 "Homily: Canonization of St Pio of Pietrelcina, Capuchin Priest," Libreria Editrice Vaticana, June 16, 2002, https://www.vatican.va/content/john-paul-ii/en/homilies/2002/documents/hf_jp-ii_hom_20020616_padre-pio.html.
281 Josefa Menendez, *The Way of Divine Love* (Westminster, MD: The Newman Press, 1950), xxiv-xxv.
282 Ibid., 212.
283 Ibid., 272.
284 Johannes Steiner, *Therese Neumann* (New York: Alba House, 1976), 19.
285 Ibid., 22.
286 Ibid., 21.
287 Ibid.
288 Ibid., 22-23.
289 Ibid., 23.
290 *Physical Phenomena*, 205.
291 Carty, *The Stigmata and Modern Science*, loc. 136 of 423.
292 Biot, *Enigma*, 39.
293 Carty, *The Stigmata and Modern Science*, loc. 142 of 423.
294 Bernard Peyrous, *Marthe Robin: A Prophetic Vision of the Gospel Message*, trans. Kathryn Spink (Dublin: Veritas Publications, 2010), 5, Kindle.
295 Ibid., 7.
296 Ibid., 10-16.
297 Ibid., 23.
298 Ibid., 30.
299 Ibid., 53-54.
300 Ibid., loc. 96 of 4710.
301 "The Unconditional Love of God for Every Individual," *Marthe Robin*, accessed August 14, 2024, https://www.martherobin.com/en/son-message/lamour-inconditionnel-de-dieu-pour-chaque-homme/.
302 Ibid., 54.
303 Ibid., 357.
304 Leo Madigan, *Alexandrina da Costa: The Mystical Martyr of Fatima* (Fatima: Ophel Books, 2010), loc. 186-211 of 1356, Kindle.
305 Ibid., loc. 889 of 1356.
306 Ibid., loc. 561 of 1356.
307 Ibid., loc. 579-583 of 1356.
308 Ibid., loc. 575 of 1356.
309 "The Story of Rhoda Wise," *Rhoda Wise House & Grotto*, accessed August 13, 2024, https://rhodawise.com/story-of-rhoda-wise/. All subsequent references from the same.
310 Raymond Arroyo, *Mother Angelica: The Remarkable Story of a Nun, Her Nerve, and a Network of Miracles* (New York: Image, 2023), 31-33.
311 Summa Theologiæ, II-II:49:8.
312 Francis of Assisi, "To All the Friars," *Writings*, trans. Robinson, 74.
313 *The Hidden Manna: A Theology of the Eucharist* (San Francisco: Ignatius Press, 2005), 259, Kindle.
314 "Message to the Eucharistic Congress at Lourdes," July 21, 1981, as cited in O'Connor, *Hidden Manna*, 9.

315 Ibid., 288.
316 Ibid., 288.
317 Antoine Imbert-Gourbeyre, *La stigmatisation, L'extase divine, et les miracles de Lourdes*, vol. 1: Les faits (Paris: L. Bellet, 1894), 67. All translations mine.
318 Joan Carroll Cruz, *Eucharistic Miracles* (Charlotte, NC: TAN Books, 2012), 243, Kindle.
319 Michael Freze, *They Bore the Stigmata* (n.p.: Michael Freze, 2016), loc. 396 of 706, Kindle.
320 Larry Peterson, "Servant of God."
321 Biot, *Enigma*, 59.
322 Ibid., 59.
323 Carl E. Schmoger, *The Life of Anne Catherine Emmerich*, vol. 1 (Rockford, IL: Tan Books and Publishers, Inc., 1976), 286-87.
324 Thurston, *Physical Phenomena*, 349-50.
325 Ibid., 289-90. All of the following quotes in this discussion reference the same citation.
326 *La stigmatisation*, 49.
327 Germanus, *Life of Saint Gemma*, 52.
328 Ibid., 212.
329 *Diary of St. Faustina*, no. 1676.
330 Ibid.
331 *Enigma*, 66.
332 Butler, *Lives*, 5020.
333 Cruz, *Eucharistic Miracles*, 258.
334 Raymond of Capua, *Life of St. Catherine*, 291.
335 Augusta Theodosia Drane, *The History of St. Catherine of Siena and Her Companions*, vol. 2 (New York: Longmans, Green, and Co., 1899), 76.
336 Thurston, *Physical Phenomena*, 145.
337 Ibid. See also Drane, *History of St. Catherine*, 2:41.
338 Emily Mary Shapcote, *Legends of the Blessed Sacrament Gathered from the History of the Church and the Lives of the Saints* (London: Burns and Oates, 1877), 106.
339 *La stigmatisation*, 247.
340 Ibid., 49.
341 *Angela of Foligno: The Passionate Mystic of the Double Abyss*, ed. Paul LaChance (Hyde Park, NY: New City Press, 2016), 48.
342 Ibid., 48-49.
343 *Diary of St. Faustina*, no. 44.
344 Ibid.
345 Capes, *St. Catherine De' Ricci*, 168.
346 Fullerton, *Life of St. Frances*, 169.
347 Drane, *History of St. Catherine*, 2:76.
348 A. Poulain, *The Graces of Interior Prayer: A Treatise on Mystical Theology*, trans. Leonora L. Yorke Smith (St. Louis: B. Herder Book Co., 1950), 291.
349 *The Spiritual Life: A Treatise on Ascetical and Mystical Theology*, trans. Herman Branderis (Tournai, Belgium: Desclee & Co., 1930), 691.
350 Ibid., 691.
351 *Interior Castle*, ed. and trans. E. Allison Peers (Mineola, NY: Dover Publications, 2007), 155, Kindle.

352 *The Graces of Interior Prayer*, 287.
353 Raymond of Capua, *Life of St. Catherine*, 99.
354 Ibid.
355 Ibid., 99-100. See also Aubrey Richardson, *The Mystic Bride: A Study of the Life-Story of Catherine of Siena* (London: T. Werner Laurie, 1911), 90.
356 Raymond of Capua, *Life of St. Francis*, 100.
357 *The Graces of Interior Prayer*, 291.
358 *Looking for a Miracle: Weeping Icons, Relics, Stigmata, Visions & Healing Cures* (Amherst, NY: Prometheus, 1993), 225.
359 *Twelve Angry Men* (London: Bloomsbury, 1996), 66.
360 "What Is the Efficient Market Hypothesis?" *Forbes Advisor*, May 11, 2022, accessed 9/13/2024, https://www.forbes.com/advisor/investing/efficient-market-hypothesis/.
361 *Black's Law Dictionary, Abridged 10th Edition*, ed. Bryan A. Garner (n.p.: Thomson Reuters, 2015), s.v. "evidence."
362 *Black's Law Dictionary*, s.v. "testimony."
363 *Black's Law Dictionary*, s.v. "cumulative testimony."
364 Michael Freze, *They Bore the Stigmata: (18th-20th Century Stigmatists)*, (No City of Publication or Publisher, 2016), loc. 166 of 706, Kindle.
365 Biot, *Enigma*, 32.
366 Gorress, *Stigmata*, 127.
367 Bret Thoman, trans. and ed., *The Diary of St. Veronica Giuliani: A Compendium: "Tell Everyone Love Has Been Found!"* 25-26, Kindle.
368 Thurston, *Physical Phenomena*, 69.
369 Ibid., 69.
370 *Black's Law Dictionary*, s.v. "document." All citations in this paragraph concern this definition.
371 *Black's Law Dictionary*, s.v. "tangible evidence."
372 *Black's Law Dictionary*, s.v. "preponderance of the evidence."
373 C.M.A. McCauliff, "Burdens of Proof: Degrees of Belief, Quanta of Evidence, or Constitutional Guarantees?" *Vanderbilt Law Review*, November 1982, https://scholarship.law.vanderbilt.edu/cgi/viewcontent.cgi?article=2891&context=vlr.
374 Robert Barron, "The Dangers of the Prosperity Gospel," April 12, 2010, https://www.wordonfire.org/articles/barron/the-dangers-of-the-prosperity-gospel/; Kate Bowler, *Blessed: A History of the American Prosperity Gospel* (New York: Oxford University Press, 2013), 11-16.
375 Bowler, *Blessed*, 7.
376 Michael Luo, "Preaching a Gospel of Wealth in a Glittery Market, New York," *The New York Times*, January 15, 2006, https://www.nytimes.com/2006/01/15/nyregion/preaching-a-gospel-of-wealth-in-a-glittery-market-new-york.html.
377 Audrey, "Joel Osteen's $10.5 Million Mansion," *Strange Buildings*, April 25, 2023, https://strangebuildings.com/joel-osteens-10-5-million-mansion/.
378 Jay Root, "Kenneth Copeland is the Wealthiest Pastor in America. So Why Does He Live in a Tax-free Texas Mansion?" *Houston Chronicle*, December 15, 2021, https://www.houstonchronicle.com/news/investigations/unfair-burden/article/kenneth-copeland-wealth-pastor-tax-free-mansion-16662283.php.
379 Ibid.

380 "Full Interview: Preacher Kenneth Copeland Defends Lavish Lifestyle," *Inside Edition*, May 20, 2019, https://www.youtube.com/watch?v=9LtF34MrsfI.
381 Bowler, *Blessed*, 234.
382 Kaycee Watchman, "Kenneth Copeland Curse of Poverty," January 8, 2013, https://www.youtube.com/watch?v=pXJp9VfgzSA.
383 C.J. Simpson, "The Stigmata: Pathology or Miracle?" BMJ 289, no. 6460 (December 1984):1746–48, https://doi.org/10.1136/bmj.289.6460.1747.
384 *Physical Phenomena*, 65.
385 Cited in Tine Van Osselaer, "Stigmata, Prophecies, and Politics."
386 Molloy, *A Visit to Louise Lateau*, 38-39.
387 Lefebvre, *Louise Lateau*, 7.
388 Ibid.
389 Molloy, *A Visit to Louise Lateau*, 17-18. See also Lefebvre, Louise Lateau, 7.
390 Wikipedia, "Gemma Galgani," accessed August 14, 2024.
391 D.H. Rawcliffe, *Occult and Supernatural Phenomena* (New York: Dover, 1959), 245.
392 Charles Mortimer Carty, *Padre Pio: The Stigmatist* (St. Paul, MN: Radio Replies Press, 1955), 283.
393 *The Cure: How Capitalism Can Save American Health Care* (New York: Encounter Books, 2006), 13.
394 "The Mercy Devotion Spreads—is Banned—and Spreads Again!" July 14, 2006, https://www.thedivinemercy.org/articles/mercy-devotion-spreads-banned-and-spreads-again.
395 Paul Johnson, *Heroes: From Alexander the Great and Julius Caesar to Churchill and de Gaulle* (No publication city or date: HarperCollins e-books), 73, Kindle Edition.
396 Ibid., 73.
397 Ibid.
398 Ibid.
399 Van Osselaer, "Stigmata, Prophecies, and Politics."
400 Biot, *Enigma*, 110.
401 *Occult and Supernatural Phenomena*, 245.
402 These remarks of Virchow were recorded in *La stigmatisée belge, Louise Lateau, histoire abrégée d'après ses biographes*, a summary of the four volumes of Canon Thierry (Brussels: de Lannoy, 1920). Cited in Biot, *Enigma*, 32.
403 Theodore G. Obenchain, *Genius Belabored*, 162. See also William J. Sinclair, *Semmelweis*, 89.
404 Sinclair, *Semmelweis*, 168.
405 Obenchain, *Genius Belabored*, 162.
406 V.K. Gupta, C. Saini, M. Oberoi, G. Kalra, M.I. Nasir, "Semmelweis Reflex: An Age-Old Prejudice," *World Neurosurgury* 136 (April 2020): e119-e125. doi: 10.1016/j.wneu.2019.12.012.
407 C.J. Simpson, "The Stigmata: Pathology or Miracle?"
408 *Physical Phenomena*, 71.
409 *The Unintended Reformation: How a Religious Revolution Secularized Society* (Cambridge, MA: The Belknap Press of Harvard University Press, 2012), loc. `1538 of 13003, Kindle.
410 *Physical Phenomena*, 52.

411 Imbert-Gourbeyre, *La stigmatisation*, 1:viii.
412 Ibid.
413 Ibid., 1:vii-viii.
414 *Bearing False Witness: Debunking Centuries of Anti-Catholic History* (West Conshohocken, PA: Templeton Press, 2016), 153, Kindle.
415 Ibid., 144.
416 Ibid.
417 *The Stanford Encyclopedia of Philosophy*, s.v. "Enlightenment," accessed August 14, 2024, https://plato.stanford.edu/entries/enlightenment/.
418 Ibid.
419 Stark, *Bearing False Witness*, 197.
420 Warren H. Carroll, *The Guillotine and the Cross* (Front Royal, VA: Christendom Press, 1991), 41.
421 Stark, *Bearing False Witness*, 194.
422 *Unintended Reformation*, loc. 1295 of 13003.
423 *Miracles, No Violations of the Laws of Nature* (London: Frank Luttmer, 1683), cited in Gregory, *Unintended Reformation*, loc. 2337 of 13003.
424 *Unintended Reformation*, loc. 1353 of 13003.
425 Ibid.
426 *Occult and Supernatural Phenomena*, 243.
427 Word Origins.com, s.v. "'hysteria/hysterical," February 10, 2021, https://www.wordorigins.org/big-list-entries/hysteria?rq=hysteria.
428 Dictionary.com, s.v. "hysteria," accessed August 14, 2024, https://www.dictionary.com/browse/hysteria.
429 Word Origins.com, "'hysteria/hysterical," February 10, 2021, https://www.wordorigins.org/big-list-entries/hysteria?rq=hysteria.
430 "The History of Hysteria in Women's Lives," *Psychology Today*, March 15, 2023, https://www.psychologytoday.com/us/blog/from-awareness-to-action/202303/the-history-of-hysteria-in-womens-lives.
431 Cecilia Tasca, Mariangela Rapetti, Mauro Giovanni Carta, and Bianca Fadda, "Women and Hysteria in the History of Mental Health," *Clinical Practice & Epidemiology in Mental Health* 8 (October 2012) doi: 10.2174/1745017901208010110.
432 Ibid.
433 Ibid.
434 Ibid.
435 Sarah Jaffray, "What is Hysteria?" Wellcome Collection, August 13, 2015, https://wellcomecollection.org/articles/W89GZBIAAN4yz1hQ.
436 *Konnersreuth: A Medical and Psychological Study of the Case of Teresa Neumann,* trans. Lancelot C. Shepphard (New York: The Macmillan Company, 1932), 115.
437 *Medical Muses: Hysteria in Nineteenth-Century Paris* (New York: W.W. Norton, 2011), 19, Kindle.
438 Ibid., 11.
439 Ibid., 14.
440 Ibid., 15.
441 Ibid., 18-19.

442 Andrew Scull, *Hysteria: The Biography* (Oxford: Oxford University Press, 2009), 105, 127.
443 Ibid., 128.
444 Hustvedt, *Medical Muses*, 27.
445 Ibid., 21-27.
446 Ibid., 45-46.
447 Ibid., 26.
448 Ibid., 29-30.
449 *Occult and Supernatural Phenomena*, 243.
450 Kasia A. Myga, Esther Kuehn, and Elena Azanon, "Autosuggestion: A Cognitive Process That Empowers Your Brain?" *Experimental Brain Research* 240 (November 2022): 382. https://www.ncbi.nlm.nih.gov/pmc/articles/PMC8858297/pdf/221_2021_Article_6265.pdf (original italics removed).
451 Ibid., 383.
452 *Saint Teresa of Ávila: A Biography* (Milwaukee: Bruce Publishing Company, 1943), 581.
453 Rohini Radhakrishnan, "What Are the 6 Stages of Rigor Mortis?" *MedicineNet*, June 25, 2024, https://www.medicinenet.com/what_are_the_stages_of_rigor_mortis/article.htm.
454 *The Incorruptibles: A Study of Incorruption in the Bodies of Various Catholic Saints and Beati* (Charlotte, NC: TAN Books, 1977), loc. 451, Kindle.
455 Ibid., loc. 533.
456 Butler, *Lives*, 4114.
457 "May in Umbria," *The Cornhill Magazine* 44, no. 262 (October 1881):446-47.
458 *The Incorruptibles*, loc. 615.
459 Tardy, *Life of Saint Clare*, 219.
460 Lloyd, *Saints*, 19.
461 *Life of Saint Clare*, 168.
462 Connolly, *Life of St. Rita*, 188.
463 Ibid., 186-87.
464 Ibid., 190-92.
465 Ibid., 264-66.
466 Ibid., 267.
467 *Biography*, 581.
468 *The Incorruptibles*, loc. 553.
469 Walsh, *Biography*, 581-82. See also Cruz, *Incorruptibles*, 162-63.
470 Helen Hester Colvill, *Saint Teresa of Ávila* (London: Methuen & Co., 1909), 321.
471 Marcelle Auclair, *Saint Teresa of Ávila*, trans. Kathleen Pond (Petersham, MA: Saint Bede's Publications, 1988), 434.
472 Colvill, *Saint Teresa of Ávila*, 322.
473 Cruz, *The Incorruptibles*, loc. 166.
474 Julen Urzika, "La canonización de santa Teresa de Jesús," *Servicio de Publicaciones de la Universidad de Navarra* 29 (2020):234.
475 Ibid., 243-44, 247.
476 Ibid., 250.
477 Ibid., 253. Translation mine.

478 "Update Regarding Remains of Sister Wilhelmina Lancaster, OSB," Diocese of Kansas City-Saint Joseph, August 22, 2024, https://kcsjcatholic.org/2024/08/update-regarding-remains-of-sister-wilhelmina-lancaster-osb/.
479 *Les stigmatisées*, 1:vii–viii.
480 *The Seven Wonders of the World: Meditations on the Last Words of Christ* (San Francisco: Ignatius Press, 1993), 69, Kindle.
481 *Cure D'Ars Today: St. John Vianney* (San Francisco: Ignatius Press, 2009), 83, Kindle.